FOLLOWING THE *Anointing*

PART II

(ORU City of Faith, Marketplace Ministry, Youth With A Mission, and Suffering)

Donald R. Tredway, MD, PhD
and
Donna J. Tredway, RN

Following the Anointing: Part II
© 2025 by Donald R. Tredway and Donna J. Tredway

Published by Insight International, Inc.
contact@freshword.com
918-493-1718

All rights reserved. No part of this book may be reproduced or transmitted in any form or by any means, electronic or mechanical, including photocopying and recording, or by any information storage and retrieval system, without permission in writing from the authors.

Unless otherwise noted all scripture quotations are taken from the New American Standard Bible. Copyright 1960, 1962, 1963, 1968, 1971, 1972, 1973, 1975, 1977, 2020 The Lockman Foundation, La Habra, CA. All rights reserved.

Scripture quotations marked (AMP) are from the Amplified Bible, Copyright 1978 by the Lockman Foundation, La Habra, CA. All rights reserved.

Scripture quotations marked (MSG) are from The Message: The new Testament, Psalms, and Proverbs. Copyright 1993, 1994, 1995, 1996, 2000, 2001, 2002 by Eugene H Peterson, NavPress Publishing Group. All rights reserved.

Scripture quotations marked (NIV) are from the New International Version. Copyright 1973, 1978, 1984 Zondervan. All rights reserved.

Scripture quotation marked (NKJV) is from the New King James Version®. Copyright © 1982 by Thomas Nelson. Used by permission. All rights reserved.

ISBN: 978-1-960452-17-7
E-Book ISBN: 978-1-960452-18-4
Library of Congress Control Number: 2025906161

Printed in the United States of America

Endorsements

Don's visits to Australia were much appreciated by the many FGBMFI Chapters throughout the Country. The highlight was his ministry at the national FGBMFI Convention in Melbourne, Victoria. His quiet message had such a powerful anointing of the Holy Spirit that many lives were changed. The presence of the Spirit was so strong that there was no need to keep proceeding with the message as the Holy Spirit was doing such a deep and wonderful work throughout the delegates.

The Word states: THEY PREACHED THE WORD WITH SIGNS FOLLOWING and that is what happened.

We thank the LORD that Don and Donna were able to fit in their many Australian visits during their busy lives. Eternity will reveal the results for His Glory.

— *David Grantham*, FGBMFI Australia

Allowing the Holy Spirit to have His way with you will change your life! That's the overwhelming message in Dr. Tredway's book *Following the Anointing, Part II*. The story he and Donna share demonstrates how the Holy Spirit never stops inviting us into adventures that we could have never imagined. As I've reconnected with Dr. Tredway in recent years, I've seen how his delight in following the Spirit's leading has never grown dim. And by both his story and his life, my own journey with the Holy Spirit has been made more alive as I continue to be amazed at all He will do. Reading this will stimulate your hunger for more of the anointing of the Spirit in your life as well."

— *Carol Tanksley*, M.D., DMin, Author
of *Overcoming Fear and Anxiety Through Spiritual Warfare* and *The Christian's Journey Through Grief*

Following the Anointing, Part II is a book not to be read quickly. Don and Donna have taken time to chronicle the last fifty years of a ministry that has touched thousands of people's lives.

The anointing of the Holy Spirit is not necessarily an evangelical term so it's not surprising that the chronicle's narrative speaks of them (Don and Donna) stumbling into the power of the Holy Spirit having come from a conservative Church background.

Don had a chronic back problem but was also at the top of his profession as an obstetrician, gynecologist, and reproductive endocrinologist. In surgery he experienced chronic pain requiring him to wear a fiberglass back brace. He attended (reluctantly) a healing meeting where his back was miraculously healed. He held high his back brace to show off to all his healing.

In *Following the Anointing,* Don and Donna were led to walk closely with people who carried a ministry of healing (people such as Ralph Wilkerson from Melodyland and Oral Roberts). This close walking with anointed people introduced a Spirit led confidence to step into new levels of the power of God.

The book is written in a way where people testify to the validity of the story being told and the healing associated with that story. Different ones personally testify to healing in their body and make the book with these personal stories and testimonies so real and authentic. The book can be devoured in a two-to-three-hour period of reading. The reader will be glued to testimony after testimony, understanding the power encounters in the power Holy Spirit.

So, get your big cup of tea/coffee ready to sit down to be personally inspired by reading, believing, and understanding the power encounters of the Holy Spirit through the eyes of Don and Donna Tredway.

— *Peter Brownhill*
Cofounder of Youth With A Mission Perth,
Western Australia

Contents

Foreword 7
Acknowledgements 11
Chapter 1: Introduction and Ramification of
Healing Testimony 13
Chapter 2: Return to Medicine, University of Oklahoma,
Tulsa Medical College 23
Chapter 3: China Trip 29
Chapter 4: City of Faith, Oral Roberts University School
of Medicine (Oral's Vision Fulfilled) 35
Chapter 5: Hillcrest Fertility Center
(Persecution and Attack) 49
Chapter 6: Ministry During Turbulent Times
(Makapala, Hawaii, and Australia FGBMFI
Melbourne Convention) 55
           Australia FGBMFI Melbourne Convention 62
Chapter 7: Loma Linda University 67
Chapter 8: Saudi Arabia (True Desert Experience) 93
Chapter 9: Kansas City and Return to Tulsa 103
Chapter 10: Working for Industry in Boston, Switzerland,
and Return to YWAM 115
           Crossroads Worship Center 118
Chapter 11: Retirement from Medicine 129
           Teaching at a Junior College 131
Chapter 12: YWAM Kona Medical Discipleship
Training Schools (MEDTS) 2012 137
           Onnuri Church Seoul, Korean 2012 (Awesome
Presence of God) and YWAM Perth, Australia 144
Chapter 13: Medical Discipleship Training School (MEDTS)
Kona 2013 151
           Onnuri Church Seoul, Korea 2013
(Manifest Love and Presence of God) 161

Chapter 14:	Recurrent Battle with Back Pain and Visitation of Jesus	163
Chapter 15:	Medical Discipleship Training School (MEDTS) Kona 2015-2017	167
	Medical Discipleship Training School (MEDTS) Kona 2017	169
Chapter 16:	Medical Discipleship Training School (MEDTS) Kona 2018, 2019, and Korean DTS	181
	Medical Discipleship Training School (MEDTS) Kona 2019 (Intense Struggles and Last School in Leadership)	193
	Korean DTS 2019	213
Chapter 17:	Medical Discipleship Training School (MEDTS) Kona 2020 (Time of Grieving) and Trip to Australia February 2020	215
	Trip to Australia 2020	217
Chapter 18:	Prostate Cancer and COVID-19 and The Prayer of Caleb	221
	The Prayer of Caleb	224
Chapter 19:	Aloha Kona Urgent Care Clinic (AKUC) and Medical Discipleship Training School (MEDTS) Kona 2021	227
	Medical Discipleship Training School (MEDTS) Kona 2021	229
Chapter 20:	The Continuing Battle with Infirmary, Heal Me Lord	233
Chapter 21:	Suffering	247
Chapter 22:	Purpose of Your Anointing from God	251
Appendix		255
	Struggling, Suffering, and Growing in the Lord	255
Bibliography		265
Author Contact		267

Foreword

There are some people who make an indelible impact on our lives. Don and Donna Tredway are two such people. I first met them in Sydney in the early eighties when I was privileged to introduce Don to Australian healthcare professionals. As a young physician, I began to understand that here was a man who could help me resolve many of the spiritual issues with which I had wrestled for years. I later travelled widely with him in China on lecture tours with the Jian Hua Foundation where I observed his utter trust and dependency on Father God and his deep personal relationship with the Holy Spirit.

In book one of this series, Don told of his early call to medical missions and subsequently, how academic pursuits had replaced God in his life. He told of his subsequent miraculous healing from incapacitating spinal disease which had nearly ended his medical career and how the anointing of the Holy Spirit at that time has changed his life and the lives of others.

In book two, Don and Donna speak of their shared experience subsequent to the anointing. They take us through the highs and

FOLLOWING THE *Anointing*: PART II

lows of their lives and how God has ministered to them through those times, strengthening them and empowering them to reach out to the lives of others. "We learned to seek His face rather than His hand," said Don. There were times when prayers seemed unanswered, and they failed to understand why God had allowed certain events to happen. Their faith was deeply challenged. Yet they understood that *"all things work together for good to those who love God, to those who are the called according to His purpose" (Rom. 8:28 NKJV).*

Don often found himself ministering in the secular marketplace where God was opening doors in the most unusual ways. These were places where the gifts of the Holy Spirit had not been seen before, and they illustrated to him God's desire to touch people in every circumstance. He began to realize that God would use him mightily, but with this came the understanding that he must move on after a short period of ministry so that God, not man, might be given the glory and that the work of the Spirit be continued through others.

He had to deal with his sense of identity, which had been based on performance rather than unconditional love. "I realized again," he said, "that I did not have to do anything to be loved by God. It's not what we do or how we perform that counts but our relationship with Him that counts." And Don challenges us. Do we have that relationship with God, and what is He saying to us right now?

As Don and Donna have shared their testimony, they have often had no idea as to how the Holy Spirit might use their ministry to bring change in the lives of others. Yet God's promise is this, *"I will give you hidden treasures, riches stored in secret places, so that you might know that I am the Lord, the God of Israel who summons you by name" (Isaiah 45:3 NIV).* Many of these treasures have been revealed at the time or, subsequently, according to God's timing.

Foreword

I recently gained some insight into this as I supported an eminent Christian doctor through a time of crisis. He had been summoned to appear before a medical tribunal to answer complaints brought against him, one of which included his stand against last-stage abortion. The questioning was long and arduous, and by the end of that day, he began to fade. As I sat with him during a break in proceedings, I had open before me a draft of this book. Don's words on the page before me were these.

> *"As I was vulnerable to minister out of my weakness, God showed me His love. All my adult life I had been the consultant, the expert witness, the one to whom people would come for expert advice. While being sued, my opinion had no validity, and I had to depend on others, especially God, for my defense. . . . I came to understand that 'out of our weakness He is glorified.' God used these times to boost me in Him so that I might endure."*
>
> *"If we are faithless, He remains faithful, for He cannot deny Himself" (2 Tim 2:13).*

I shared these words with my friend, and he was greatly encouraged. The results that day were in his favor.

I recommend this book without reservation to all who seek a deeper personal relationship with God. As you read, you will grow in knowledge and understanding of the Grace and the Spirit of God. "Come with us," says Don, "as we walk through the second stage of our journey in following His anointing."

— *Dr. Ernest Frank Crocker*, BSc (Med)
MBBS FRACP DDU FAANMS
New South Wales Chair, Christian Medical
and Dental Fellowship of Australia

Acknowledgements

To our four daughters (Tammy, Jennifer, Kimberly, and Noel) who have walked through some of these experiences with us and witnessed the resulting challenges, struggles, and blessings.

We also want to acknowledge all of the people who have prayed for us and financially supported us during these years. In addition, we want to thank those who have added inserts into Part I and Part II of our story. Quite often, they witnessed the Lord and His presence doing more than Donna and I could have ever imagined.

I, Don, also want to thank my wife, Donna, for standing beside me all these years. Her support and encouragement were instrumental in my journey with the Lord. This is also a part of her story in *Following the Anointing, Part I* and *Part II*. Quite often she would stay in the background, leaving the public ministry to me while she ministered one-on-one. The depth of her ministry and discernment is profound. The anointing of the Lord is so much stronger during the times we are ministering together. In addition to her inserts in this book, I appreciate her editing skills of my verbose nature.

FOLLOWING THE *Anointing*: PART II

I also want to acknowledge the encouragement, mentorship, and friendship that Dr. Bruce Thompson has had upon my life in understanding the love of God. Thank you, Bruce, for exemplifying the Lord's character so profoundly in life. While writing Part II of our story, Dr. Bruce has had the ultimate healing by going home to the Lord. We miss you, Bruce, and look forward to seeing you again.

Finally, both Donna and I want to acknowledge the faithfulness of God and thank Him for revealing Himself to us in a very tangible and meaningful way as we tried to follow His voice. In addition, I, Don, want to also affirm the Lord's unfailing love.

CHAPTER 1

Introduction and *Ramification* of Healing Testimony

This is part two of the path that my wife, Donna, and I have had in following our Lord Jesus Christ. This continued story will show not only our failures, struggles, suffering, and pain but also the faithfulness and loving kindness of God. It is not our intention to write about ourselves, but about the Lord and His anointing that is available to all obedient servants who walk with Him. To that end, we will share, along with others, our various perspectives as to what the Lord has done in our lives and others through His Anointing. As you read, let faith grow in your heart. Seek His face, be transformed by the Holy Spirit, and let God's glory be manifest in you. Let this book encourage you to grow in the Lord and allow the Holy Spirit to guide you in taking other people into God's presence. Following Him releases tremendous joy, peace, and love. I pray that you will come to a new understanding of God the Father and His tremendous love for each one of us. As you become secure in Him and know Him as Aba Father, you will be released into all that He has for you.

In part one of our journey,[1] we shared with you my story as a physician called to medical missions as a teenager, but medicine and education replaced God. While in the Navy, I had three back surgeries that failed, and I was going to be discharged from the Navy with a total disability. I walked into a healing service at Melodyland Christian Center in California in 1977 where God healed me and filled me with the Holy Spirit when I did not believe in either. The pastor of Melodyland, Ralph Wilkerson, became my mentor as I was released into ministry through Melodyland and FGBMFI (Full Gospel Business Men's Fellowship International). I went from the Navy to the University of Chicago to Oral Roberts University's School of Medicine in its founding days and was sent by Grace Fellowship Church in Tulsa to the mission field with Youth With A Mission (YWAM) in Kona, HI. With YWAM and FGBMFI, my family and I went to the mission fields of Australia, New Zealand, Malaysia, China, and Indonesia. The first part of our journey deals with this part of our life in following His anointing.[1] The first part of our story also included some of the pivotal teaching that the Holy Spirit released us to share worldwide.

Chronologically in Part II as well as Part I,[1] we have added inserts from others describing what they witnessed the Holy Spirit doing. My healing not only changed my life but also changed the life of others. The following detailed insert is from a neighbor who witnessed my healing. See how the sharing of my testimony changed his life so that he could begin his walk with the Lord and be released into ministry.

Introduction and *Ramification* of Healing Testimony

Rick Gamble: April 7, 1977, God Heals Dr. Don Tredway...and I was SHOCKED! In October 1975, my family moved to Hayward, CA across the street and two houses away from where the Tredways lived. We had three boys, the Tredways had four girls, and we soon became friends. Of course, I had no idea what God had in mind. On a Sunday morning as we were getting ready to go to All Saints Catholic Church, my wife Sharon said, "I'm taking the boys to Neighborhood Church in Castro Valley." I responded, "You can't do that, we're Catholics." She did it anyway. I went to the Catholic Church, but it was the last time. I realized being with my family was more important.

As we started going regularly to the now non-denominational church, I saw the Tredways there as well. In early 1977, Dr. Tredway mentioned he was going to have back surgery at Oak Knoll Naval Hospital in Oakland, which was where he worked. At one point I went and visited him at the hospital after his surgery, and he didn't look good; his surgery was not successful. Don's diagnosis was not a promising one.

During that period, I was the Athletic Director and Basketball coach at Alameda High School in Alameda, California. I was very busy, so I didn't know what was going on in the house across the street. When I found out, my life started to change quickly.

I had just gotten home from school and was playing a game with one of our boys when Donna Tredway knocked on our door and just walked in the house. Donna announced, "God has healed Don, and he is giving his testimony tomorrow at 6:00 p.m. at our home, and you are invited." I said nothing at first. After Donna left, I told Sharon, "I can't go there tomorrow. God doesn't heal anyone now. That only happened 2,000 years ago!" Sharon responded, "Is Don your friend?" I said, "Yes." She said, "He won't be if you don't listen to his testimony." I said, "I'm going!"

What I saw and heard was shocking. It shook me to the core. He was upright, walking around, and feeling normal. I had already prayed to receive Jesus and be born again, but God is still healing people. I was forced to reevaluate what I believed. I started reading my Bible even more. I had to rethink everything.

When we heard the Tredways were moving, we were all disappointed. But Donna made one more appearance at our house that allowed God to make His move in my life in a BIG way. I had asthma since I was five years old, and pneumonia twice as an adult. I was taking shots, prescriptions, and using an inhaler, all to help me breathe. So, for a thirty-three-year-old man, I wasn't doing well. Donna walked into our house and said, "God wants to heal you, but you have to travel to Melodyland, where Don received his healing." I said nothing. I told Sharon, "I can't go now; I'm very busy at school." So, I put it off for a couple of months.

One day I received a note in my school mailbox from my principal. The note said the school was sending me to Anaheim, CA to the California State Athletic Directors Conference. Coincidently, it was two blocks from Melodyland, where the Healing Service was to happen on Thursday morning at 10:00. My conference ended on Wednesday afternoon. So, I went to the Healing Service! My parents were visiting my sister in nearby Diamond Bar. They picked me up, and the three of us planned to go together to the Healing Service and have lunch after, before dropping me off at John Wayne Airport.

Donna had told me, "If you go, God is going to change your life!" I arrived at 9:30 a.m. for the 10:00 a.m. service. Donna had said about 3,500 people would be there. I looked at the round stage

Introduction and *Ramification* of Healing Testimony

and picked a spot which was in the middle of a section where Pastor Ralph Wilkerson could not see me unless he turned around and looked to the area behind him. The service was to last about two hours. By 11:30 a.m. when I looked at my watch, I thought it was almost over. We had wasted our time. At 11:35 a.m. it became totally silent. I thought, nothing is happening. At that point Pastor Wilkerson turned to his right, looked toward my section, and said, "God has brought someone a long way. Stand up. He is going to change your life!" I froze. He then repeated it again. I thought I would peek behind me to see if anyone was standing. Nobody had stood up. Then the pastor said, "The man in the blue shirt looking behind him, please stand up. God has brought you here to change your life." I stood up, and I really don't know what was prayed after that. My head got very warm. The heat traveled all the way to my feet, and down I went, "slain in the Spirit." I was lying on the floor for a long time. I couldn't get up.

Later during lunch my mother said, "I thought you died, what happened?" I took my inhaler out of my pocket and put it on the table. I reached for my prescription in my other pocket, placed it alongside the inhaler and said, "If this was really God, I won't need any of this ever again. Forty-seven years later, I NEVER needed them again. God changed my life.

Rick Gamble: After Melodyland: Over the next four years, God moved in many ways. I started teaching a Bible Study weekly. We changed churches, which opened the door to preaching on Sundays as a fill-in at the Lighthouse Christian Center. Later, when the pastor resigned to take another position, I was asked to bring the Sunday message more than thirty times before I was offered the position full time. I turned it down because God was leading our family to

FOLLOWING THE *Anointing*: PART II

Kailua Kona, Hawaii to join YWAM. And who was there? Dr. Don Tredway and Donna.

After eight months at YWAM taking Discipleship Training and Counseling classes, Don asked me to travel to Southeast Asia[1] to share the gospel of Jesus to that part of the world. I was excited to go because Don's ministry glorified God wherever he shared the gospel. On our way to Malaysia, we first stopped in Singapore. Don spoke at a church service on a Sunday morning. Later in the week, what I remember the most about ministry in Singapore took place in a large auditorium. It was there I shared my testimony for the first time. Don Tredway spoke as the main speaker. At the end of the meeting, he invited people who needed prayer to come forward. What I witnessed during that time of prayer was something I had never seen before; little did I know, I would see it many more times in Malaysia. I started praying for people on the right side of the auditorium. I had no idea what was transpiring elsewhere. It seemed normal at first, but more and more and more people were coming forward. At that point the Holy Spirit swept through the crowd. People seeking prayer never made it to the front. They were "slain in the Spirit" in numbers I had never seen anywhere before. God was "moving for His Glory." He didn't need us. People were saved, people were healed, and lives were changed forever...and mine was one of them. Praise the name of Jesus!

We spent the most time in Malaysia. We had several meetings, and God was glorified every time. People later asked me, "Isn't Malaysia a Muslim Country?" It was in 1982, but we had freedom to minister. The Holy Spirit preceded us wherever we went. After several meetings in the city of Kuala Lumpur, we headed 148 km to Malacca, both in Malaysia. What happened there was also unforgettable. The first night our host drove us to a building on a dirt road.

Introduction and *Ramification* of Healing Testimony

It had no bathrooms or running water, but it did have a generator. Looking back, I think 125 people were there. We had an interpreter, who translated what we spoke in English into the local language. After I gave my testimony and Dr. Tredway shared the Word of God, he called for those who wanted prayer. Near the end of prayer time, the interpreter gathered twelve people together who said they wanted to receive Jesus. I had the interpreter organize everyone in a circle, we prayed, and they were "born again." One of the twelve was in a wheelchair. He had spent the last twenty years unable to walk. I prayed for God to heal him, but at that moment nothing happened. Later that night when everyone went home, the man in the wheelchair was lying in his bed when he felt this heat start at the top of his head and move all the way throughout his body to the bottom of his feet. God had healed him.

The next night as we drove down the dirt road toward the building where the meeting was to take place again, we realized something was going on. The crowd was everywhere; the building was full. I asked the doctor who was driving us, "What's going on?" He replied, "They have come to see the Power of God." When we got into the building, we gathered in a circle to pray. Our prayer was interrupted by what we in the USA would describe as a "roar of the crowd." The man in the wheelchair walked in carrying his wheelchair above his head and told everyone Jesus had healed him. Although this occurred forty-two years ago, I can see it like it happened yesterday.

The next day we took a four-hour car ride back to Kuala Lumpur. The following Friday we were at a meeting that I referred to as an "Upper Room." (This was the last meeting Don and I were together before he traveled to China). I was to give my testimony, and then Don would give the main message. Before I even finished, I turned to Don and said, "The Holy Spirit is here." He got up and called people to come forward for prayer. The Spirit moved, the people were "slain in the Holy Spirit," and God received the glory like He always deserves.

On Sunday, Don had already gone to China. I went to a church service on the top floor of the hotel at which we were staying. The owner of the hotel had converted to Christianity, and the top floor of the hotel became a church for Sunday service which housed close to 1,000 people. The guest speaker that day was from Indonesia. His message was very good. Before closing the service, the church pastor turned to me and asked if I had anything to share. I said I did. I shared with the church that I knew many of them had been treated very poorly by their family when they turned to Jesus. But I also knew they had not forgiven their family for the way they were treated. It was time to repent and forgive. I had seen the number "6" in my head as a white block number before I got up to share. I honestly thought 6 people would come forward to ask for forgiveness and receive prayer. I was so wrong! It was closer to 600, NOT 6! I was stunned; it was overwhelming at first. But the Holy Spirit spoke. All the leaders of the church got up to pray with me. Most of the people coming forward never made it to the front. The Holy Spirit moved through the room like a powerful rushing wind. People were rejoicing, but most were on the floor, slain by the Power of God. I thought, "Could Pentecost had been any better than this?" Prayer seemed to go on and on. One thing I can say is, when the service was over, I was totally exhausted!

I remember thinking, "Don Tredway has a real calling by God. To be a blessing to the people he ministers to year after year, only God and His Spirit could keep Don healthy enough to keep going."

Introduction and *Ramification* of Healing Testimony

Don: Rick's testimony is a fulfillment of:

Revelation 12:11 And they overcame him because of the blood of the Lamb and because of the word of their testimony, and they did not love their life even when faced with death.

As I shared my testimony of what God had done in my life,[1] I had no idea how the Holy Spirit will use it in others' lives. Rick's story emphasis this point and the fulfillment of this scripture in his life and the lives of others. **As you read Rick's insert, is the Lord speaking to you to share your testimony and begin to be released into the ministry that He has for you?**

The second part of our story is a continuation of our testimony of how the Lord led us after leaving full-time ministry with YWAM. It was difficult to leave full-time ministry because of witnessing what the Lord was doing through the powerful signs and wonders that Rick described. At this time, however, the Lord reminded me that my identity in Him was that of being a physician. In this part of our story, the Lord released me into a **marketplace ministry** at the University of Oklahoma, Oral Roberts University (ORU) City of Faith, and Loma Linda University, as a visiting YWAM teacher, through practice in the middle east, private practice, and the Biotech Industry, as a Biotech consultant and a professor at a community college, and finally in a retired status. As in full-time ministry, noted in Part I,[1] the Holy Spirit would continue to open amazing doors of ministry using my identity as an academic physician.

Come walk with us through the pages of this second part of our journey in following His anointing. His Holy Spirit led us through challenges and struggles, but we witnessed tremendous releases

FOLLOWING THE *Anointing*: PART II

in people's lives as we followed His voice even during our times of struggles and pain. **Is this a marketplace journey that the Lord is speaking about to you also?**

CHAPTER 2

Return to Medicine, University of *Oklahoma*, Tulsa Medical College

Shortly before God's revelation of His unconditional love to me,[1] I was in Singapore and sat next to an Anglican Bishop at a banquet. He turned to me and said, "God is calling you back to Medicine." I couldn't believe it. I thought that I had left medicine behind me. Recall that the year before I had tried to return to the University of Chicago when the Lord ask me to humble myself before my former chairman to correct some wrongs. I was not given the opportunity to go back at that time and remained very fulfilled in ministry with YWAM. I did, however, begin to have a sense that I would be returning to medicine at some point, and the word from the bishop confirmed what I was sensing. **An important principal to remember is that a prophetic word should confirm what the Lord is speaking to you.**

FOLLOWING THE *Anointing*: PART II

Shortly afterward, I attended a medical meeting in Dallas, met a member of the program, and was asked to apply for the Chairmanship of the Department of Obstetrics and Gynecology at the University of Oklahoma, Tulsa Medical College. The University had a 3rd and 4th year medical student clerkship program in Tulsa in addition to a four-year residency program in association with the three local Tulsa hospitals (St. John, St. Francis, and Hillcrest). I had met the faculty and clinical members of the department while working in Tulsa at ORU. I applied, had some interviews, and was offered the position. During the process of interviewing, I visited the University of Oklahoma in Oklahoma City and was also offered a position as Section Chief of Reproductive Endocrinology and Infertility at the main campus of the University of Oklahoma in Oklahoma City. Our house and church, as well as the presence of ORU (along with its disappointments)[1], were in Tulsa, and we felt the Lord was directing us to return there. We would rent our house in Kona, Hawaii to other YWAMers.

We returned to Tulsa in 1982, and I was Professor and Chairman of the Department of Obstetrics and Gynecology at the University of Oklahoma, Tulsa Medical College. I essentially had four bosses – the University and the three local hospitals. The program was on probation at the time, and I had a year to reorganize it in order to maintain accreditation. Academically, this seems to be how I am used by God. I would go into areas and establish programs and then after a certain period of time would transition to somewhere else. I would be with the university for two years until 1984.

As I look back on my walk with the Lord, I can see how He has used me in a similar manner spiritually. Call it pioneering, if you will. God would have me minister in meetings where gifts of the Spirit had not been seen before in order to release and demonstrate

Return to Medicine, University of *Oklahoma*, Tulsa Medical College

His desire to touch the people. In situations where people began to look to the man instead of God, I knew it was time to move on so that God could bring in others to release the Holy Spirit in order that He might get the Glory.

We returned to our home near ORU and to our church, Grace Fellowship. Pastor Bob Yandian was teaching on Mephibosheth and the blood covenant[2] in **2 Samuel 9**. It was just what I needed to prepare me for the next phase of my life. I would suggest reading this story if you feel you are unworthy to be a son or daughter at the King's table (see the section on Jesus the Friend in the appendix on the character of God, part one of our story).[1] I missed the large evangelistic meetings and moving in the power of the Holy Spirit. I even questioned whether I had missed God. One day during my devotion time, I prayed and asked if I had. I heard Him speak to my mind, **"Don, not one person has to be healed or saved by My Spirit through you for you to be loved by Me."** God was still dealing with me about my identity and acceptance in Him being based upon performance instead of unconditional love. I realized again that I did not have to do anything to be loved by God! Thank you, Father, for your unconditional love and the security that results. **Ministry will come out of a relationship with Him!**[3-7]

> **1 Corinthians 13:1-2** If I speak with the tongues of men and of angels, but do not have love, I have become a noisy gong or a clanging cymbal. If I have the gift of prophecy and know all mysteries and all knowledge; and if I have all faith, so as to remove mountains, but do not have love, I am nothing.

How hard it was for me to come to that understanding. It is so easy to fall back into the performance mode and the pride of life. It is not what we do (perform) for God, but it is our relationship with Him that He desires. As we have relationship with Him, the ministry of Jesus will flow out of this relationship. **Do you have that relationship with Him? Is He speaking to you now?**

In November of 1981, while we were in Hawaii with YWAM, the City of Faith (COF) opened and began seeing patients in a Gynecology Department. There was no Obstetrical Department. Upon returning to Tulsa, I had to pass by the COF every morning and evening on my way to and from work at the University of Oklahoma. For the next two years as I drove by the COF building, I would thank the Lord, in faith, for the obstetrical unit.

I had a private practice in addition to the academic teaching as OU faculty. It was good seeing patients again. I was able to pray for those who wanted prayer and to walk alongside others in seeking God as to how He wanted to treat them – through prayer, medicine, or often a combination of the two.

In Singapore I had met Professor Chuck Farrer from the School of Theology at ORU. He invited me to speak at his church in north Tulsa where the meetings were like the ones overseas in that the Lord's presence moved mightily in ministering to the people. I enjoyed ministry, but now it seemed as if the Lord asked me to set it aside. For the next few years, it seemed as if I was in a closet and God would let me out from time to time to minister in local churches. I recall one female resident that was quite a challenge because of her lifestyle. A few years later I met her at a medical dinner/meeting and happened to sit next to her at dinner. I noticed that she said grace before her meal, to which I was surprised. She noticed my reaction and related an interesting story. She told me that before I came to the University of Oklahoma, the residents had heard about my being at ORU and in the mission field. She said, "I watched you, and because of your witness, I sought the Lord in a time of need in my life and accepted the Lord Jesus Christ as my savior. I want to thank you for your silent witness." I was floored! While I thought nothing was happening, there was a witness without even knowing it.

I continued to build my private practice and the residency program at the university. Since the residency program was on probation when I came, my job was to achieve accreditation by correcting the deficiencies. I had to work with the three hospitals and the University, and I was able to bring the program into correction and received full accreditation a year after I arrived.

During my time at the university, Hillcrest Hospital hired a clinician and an andrologist/ embryologist to start an In Vitro Ferritization Center (IVF) in Tulsa. The clinician had completed his residency at Eastern Virginia Medical School and had done a rotation in an In Vitro Fertilization service in the Department of Obstetrics and Gynecology under the direction of Georgiana and Howard Jones. The Jones were pioneers in Reproductive Endocrinology and Gynecology who had left their tenured positions at John Hopkins University to join the faculty at Eastern Virginia University and start the first IVF Center in the US.

Both individuals were on my faculty at the university in Tulsa, and it was exciting to be a part of the beginning of the Hillcrest Infertility Center. I was associated with the center as its certified Reproductive Endocrinologist, and it was the second IVF Center in the US. Those were the early days of IVF, and we all rejoiced when our first IVF baby was born.

IVF is an area that I had wanted to be involved in when I was doing my training at USC in the mid '70s, but the ethics board of the hospital would not let us get into this area. This area was very fulfilling for me, and a close friendship developed with the two doctors and myself. The embryologist and his wife became close friends, and we often played bridge together in our homes. Our relationships would be tested and strained and is to this day, as I will share with you later.

God opened doors for me to be involved in the early ethical discussions of this new area, Assisted Reproductive Techniques in Reproductive Endocrinology, where fertilization occurs in the laboratory outside of the human body.

CHAPTER 3

China Trip

One evening I was invited to a local Christian ophthalmologist's home where I met Dr. Donald and Penny Dale. Dr. Dale and his wife were former medical missionaries to China and were now taking Christian physicians into China on short-term teaching outreaches to Chinese physicians. This was done through a Christian group in Hong Kong, the Jian Hua Foundation.

My meeting Dr. Dale resulted in traveling with him and a nuclear medicine colleague from Australia, Dr. Ern Crocker, to China from June 19-July 2, 1982. We met at Dr. Dale's home in Hong Kong and there also met Dr. Jonathan Ho, a cardiologist from Hong Kong, for our short-term medical teaching trip to Changsha, China. The day before we were to leave, Dr. Dale received correspondence from our Chinese host in Changsha, advising us not to come. We prayed and all of us felt that in faith we should go. At the airport we were told that there were no available seats on the plane even though we had tickets. Dr. Dale argued with the airlines ticket counter representative, and we waited and prayed. At the last minute, we were given seats and boarded the plane to China. We flew that day from Hong Kong into an airport in China (I don't recall the site) where we arrived late and had to stay overnight. The airport had Chinese MIG airplanes from the '50s on the runways, and Chairman Mao banners hung all over the main building. Armed Chinese soldiers were present as we walked, and spiritually it was very cold. We found our accommodations for the night, which consisted of a hard tatami mat with no pillow. The next morning at the ticket counter we again were told that there were no seats available on the plane to Changsha. What a spiritual battle we were in. Dr. Dale again argued with the ticket counter representative, and at the last minute we were given seats to fly to Changsha. It was an interesting flight because some of the Chinese had chickens with them in cages that they placed in the overhead. When we landed in Changsha (the home of Chairman Mao Tse-Tung), we were meet by a physician and the political official. We learned that the physician was a Christian and had been told to cancel our meeting by the officials. When we arrived, they had to host us, and everything was being prepared at the last minute. We were taken to the hotel, and Dr. Dale advised us to be careful of our conversations in the rooms because they would most likely contain listening and recording devices. (This was in the early days when the Chinese Communists first opened the doors to westerners.) We met other western businessmen who met with officials and related how long it took to build relations and establish a business with the Chinese.

We began the next day teaching, each in our area of expertise. I had thought they would want to hear about contraception but no, they wanted to hear about IVF and infertility. This was during the time when the Communist government imposed the one-child rule which was so contrary to Chinese culture. Consequently, if you were infertile, it was a significant issue. So, I taught mainly on

China Trip

Reproductive Endocrinology and Infertility (I started my lectures with pictures of the facility in Tulsa, which the Chinese found quite interesting). Dr. Ern Crocker taught on Nuclear Medicine, and Dr. Jonathan Ho taught on Cardiology. The first day the interpreter was having difficulty interpreting, and a senior Chinese doctor in the group of about fifty physicians stopped the lecture. We took a break, and at the end of the break we had a new translator. It had been a while since I had taught with a translator, which required quite an adjustment. In the evening, we would walk on the street with Dr. Dale without the political official, and local Chinese would come up to us wanting to speak English. Dr. Dale introduced us to a food vendor along the road, and I certainly prayed over the food before eating it. One evening a young man asked us to tell him who Jesus was. The country was spiritually void of the gospel.

One evening we were invited to the home of the local physician for a meal. He was a surgeon who had been in charge of the hospital when the communists took over and was imprisoned for seven years before being released. His wife was an ophthalmologist, and we were their first foreign guests since the cultural revolution. The political official also accompanied us to the dinner. It was a wonderful meal with his wife and family. The physician had a small old organ that he played after dinner as we all sang Christian songs. I will never forget when we sang "Onward Christian Soldiers," the political official became excited and sang along "Solidarity Forever," which was to the same melody. It was such a witness to me to see Christians who have endured prison for their faith. Thank you, Lord, for your faithful servants.

We had taken an overhead projector as a gift to the institution, but they would not accept it. Dr. Dale explained that if they had accepted it, it would indicate that the government could not give them what they needed – another encounter with the Asian concept of "losing face." I fell in love with Asia and felt that I was seeing it through the eyes of the Lord instead of as I did when in the Navy during my Viet Nam experience. This was an exciting trip which would subsequently result in multiple teaching trips to China.

Back in Tulsa I continued my work at the University and Hillcrest Fertility Center. I was contacted by the 700 Club in 1982 and also the FGBMFI. A film crew came to Tulsa and interviewed me and my family about my healing. It was aired nationally on the 700 Club TV program, and my testimony was published in the FGBMFI Voice magazine. To God be the glory for the doors that He was opening while I was in a marketplace ministry. God was opening doors in most unusual ways.

When we had returned to Tulsa, the situation at ORU had changed. The Dean with whom I had a conflict at ORU School of Medicine had left, and the new Dean, Dr. David Hinshaw (former dean of Loma Linda University in Los Angeles), contacted me about returning to ORU. I met with him a few times, and he was interested in what we had been doing on the mission field. Since Loma Linda was established to train medical missionaries for the Seventh Day Adventist Church, he was wanting to hear what we had been doing. Donna and I got to know David and his wife Mildred, a precious couple who we liked very much. We would see each other socially and visit in each other's home and also shared some of the VHS tapes we had from our overseas ministry. They were interested in the Holy Spirit and speaking in tongues and enjoyed seeing the supernatural manifestation of God on the tapes. They shared about the charismatic branch of the Adventist Church, although most churches were denominational with no freedom in the Holy Spirit.

China Trip

Although we had a wonderful relationship, without an obstetrical unit at the COF, I did not feel a release to return to ORU.

In 1983 Donna and I were to return to China for two weeks with a medical teaching team with Dr. Don Dale. I was scheduled to teach at the University of Peking, but the Chinese government changed their mind when we arrived in Hong Kong. There was political unrest in China, and they revoked our entry visas. Donna and I had a two-week vacation in Hong Kong. I was able to teach at the YWAM base and at the University of Hong Kong. I recall doing teaching rounds at the university and asking the doctors in training about alternate ways to treat different conditions. At that time there was only one way to treat, and that was the way the Professor Chairman dictated. Medical education can vary so much depending upon the mentors.

In June of 1989 I taught at a retreat for the new residents in ORU's family practice program. They had a weeklong spiritual retreat nearby Tulsa to prepare them for the residency. I taught on Spiritual Warfare, Curses, and the Authority of the Believer. Again, the Lord revealed himself.

CHAPTER 4

City of *Faith*, Oral Roberts University School of Medicine (Oral's Vision Fulfilled)

One day God answered my prayers concerning an obstetrical unit at the COF. After two years of praying in the morning and evening as I drove by the hospital thanking God for the obstetric unit, someone donated the money to open one. I was excited when this was announced but also disappointed since I would not be a part of it. Then one Sunday morning while I was shaving and getting ready to go to our church, Grace Fellowship, the Lord spoke to my mind and told me to go to Billy Joe Daugherty's Victory Christian Center's Sunday morning service which was held at ORU's Mabee Center. The rest of the family went on to our home church, and I went to Victory. As I walked in, there was a last-minute change in the speaker. It was Oral Roberts. I am not sure what he spoke about that day for God was speaking to me about returning to ORU to become chairman again and to establish the obstetrical unit. At the end of the service, I went forward to speak to Oral. That usually was hard to do because of Oral's bodyguards, but there were none that day. Before I could say anything, he looked at me and said, "Do what God is telling you to do," and he walked away before I could say anything.

Unfortunately, Dean Hinshaw had left the COF and returned to Loma Linda to become President of the Medical Center. While the dean's position was open, I contacted the Provost, Dr. Winslow, sharing with him what the Lord and others had previously spoken to me before about being dean. He informed me that they had selected a faculty member, an infectious disease specialist, Dr. Edwards. Subsequently, I contacted Dr. Edwards and shared with him my experience with Oral and talked to him about the department. I inquired if he was open to developing a city-wide residency program in Obstetrics and Gynecology with the University of Oklahoma and the other hospitals. I had discussed this with some of my OU faculty who were supportive. Dr. Edwards was open since they only had two gynecologists, but when I approached the dean at OU, he was not supportive of a combined program because of the local animosity that was caused when Oral built the COF. At the beginning of the school of medicine at ORU, there had been an agreement to use the existing hospitals for their students. With the confirmation of that Sunday when Oral spoke to me, I eventually resigned my position, still believing that a combined program would be best. I returned to ORU and the COF in October1984 after being at OU for two years.

The COF only had two gynecologists, Dr. Herb Gates and Dr. Joy King (a former resident of mine from the University of Chicago), both of whom had contracts to only practice gynecology. In an academic setting and as chairman, I could have asked them to change or leave if they would not comply. When I prayed about the situation, the Lord said to honor their contracts. They were relieved when I told them their contracts would be honored, and they agreed to cover the ER for gynecologic emergencies while I recruited more faculty and established the obstetrical unit. I worked with the head nurse, Denise Satarawalla, in developing the birthing center and the Standard Operating Procedures (SOPs) so that the patient would deliver in the same room in which they labored (not the usual practice at that time). I also wanted to develop a nurse midwife service. I had tried to start a midwife program at OU, but it was not supported by the local obstetricians and hospitals. I was ahead of my time in Oklahoma although we had such programs in California and in other areas of the country. I brought my well-established medical practice from OU to the COF, building out the obstetrical unit, and began looking for staff to establish a well-rounded department. As I prayed about recruiting, the Lord told me not to advertise but that He would bring people. I had a Department Administrator, Ed Seibert, who was very helpful during this time. Kitty White became my administrative assistant. Kitty had been the administrative assistant for the Chairman of the Department of Medicine, Dr. Joe Linhardt, when I had been at ORU before going to YWAM. Kitty became a close personal friend of the family and would be with me for a number of years in various capacities.

The OB unit was opened by Oral and Evelynn Roberts with much fanfare on his television program, and the first baby was born on 22 October 1984. In order to meet the clinical demands and the call schedule, two local Christian Ob/Gyn physicians who I knew from OU, Drs. Brian Hall and Richard Glick, agreed to help us for a few months until we were fully staffed. When they were on call at the COF and tied up at another hospital with their own practice, I would go in for them. Dr. Betsy Neuenschwander, who I had interviewed in 1980, joined me in the spring of 1985 to help with the obstetrical private practice. She also ran the student clerkship program and helped develop the obstetrical practice.

Betsy and I would eventually run the obstetrical service for the first year with ten to fifteen deliveries a month. (It would be a year before others would be released to join us.) We also covered the family practice program by backing their residents and staff that delivered approximately twenty-five patients per month. Betsy and I were very busy and were on call every other night. When one of us was away, we essentially had to stay in the hospital. It was a very tiring but also very exciting time. (Betsy's husband, Mark, was a trained family practice physician/surgeon and also worked at the COF.) Dr. Jeremiah Whittington, a Christian physician at the Claremore Indian Public Health Service Hospital, called me about coming to the COF. I had known Dr. Whittington since 1983 from doing a weekly fertility clinic at the Indian Hospital. Dr. John MacFarland, a Christian and recent graduate from an OB/GYN program in Texas, and his wife Raquel visited us in Tulsa and felt that God was calling them to the COF. A nurse midwife, Charlotte Gish from the Public Health Department of the State of Oklahoma, who I had worked with at OU, also felt called of God to join us. She helped me establish a midwife service at COF. Two other midwives were hired as well. This was one of the first nurse midwife programs in the state of Oklahoma. The Lord had spoken to me that just as in the time of Moses, midwives were blessed by Him and He would bless a midwife service.

> **Exodus 1:20-21** So God was good to the midwives, and the people multiplied, and became very mighty. Because the midwives feared God, He established households for them.

I was also contacted by a Canadian physician originally from Montreal, Dr. Aikman, who was practicing in Hilo, Hawaii. He and his wife felt that the Lord was speaking to them about going to ORU. This was exciting because not only was he trained as an Obstetrician/Gynecologist, but he was also a certified midwife. At this time, I went on vacation for a week from the COF to teach at a counseling school in Makapala on the Big Island of Hawaii. I drove over to Hilo and met Dr. Robert Aikman and his wife Bobbie at his birthing center. It is interesting how the Lord had prepared the way in the relationship with Bob. He was familiar with me from my previous time with YWAM on the Kona side of the island. Three years earlier I had ministered at a healing service sponsored by Calvary Community Church at the King Kamehameha hotel in Kona. I had prayed for one of his patients who God healed and who later shared about her healing with Bob. After this meeting with Bob and his wife, the Lord confirmed that Bob was to be the head of obstetrics and the midwife service. It was exciting to see the Lord recruiting.

The Lord provided excellent trained nurses and clinic help as we built our staff. Michelle Disc, a nurse friend from YWAM, Glenda McKinney, and a nurse practitioner joined the clinic staff. Glenda was a former Miss Tennessee with a dynamite personality and became our head nurse. Under her clinical leadership, the clinic hummed. From the north side of Tulsa from Buddy Harrison's (son-in-law of Kenneth Hagen) church, our clinic administrator Yolanda Waller also joined and brought a friend, Renee McCullough, from the same church to be our receptionist. Renee and Yolanda became our prayer warriors for the clinics and the patients. I watched God bring all the staff into our clinic on the 39th floor in clinic tower. The clinic had two sides with a receptionist for both sides. In regard to the receptionist beside Renee, I have an interesting story. One Sunday after church the family and I went out for Sunday brunch to a buffet in a nearby Sheraton Hotel. Jennifer Priester came to our table to say hello. She had recently been referred to Donna for counseling. As she was introducing herself, the Lord spoke to me to hire her for the open receptionist position. She was a waitress and had no experience in healthcare. It did not make sense to me, but there was no doubt what the Lord was speaking. I told her to come and apply and set up an appointment for her to be interviewed by Dr. Gates. Dr. Gates came to me after the interview questioning why I wanted her for the position. I shared with him the story of the Lord speaking to me. We hired her on the Word of the Lord. Dr. Gates trained her for the receptionist position, and he also became a substitute father for her. Jennifer became a valued employee and member of the team. Over the next few years, I witnessed the healing power of God in Jennifer's life. To complete the clinic staff, we had a Methodist minister assigned to our clinic floor that was available to minister to patients and staff. Whole person medicine was being practiced with ministry to Spirit, Soul, and Body. We believed in the supernatural, and the gifts of the Spirit were evident. This was the fulfillment of Oral's vision of the combination of prayer and medicine.

At the dedication of the obstetrical unit, Richard and Lindsay Roberts announced that Lindsay was pregnant. She would later deliver at the COF Obstetrical Unit in 1985. A perinatologist friend in Tulsa delivered their child since he had delivered their first baby a year earlier who died in the neonatal unit. I later had the privilege of delivering their third child. Although Richard would later have controversaries after taking over for his father at the university, he and his wife Lindsay were gracious patients for which to care. I also had the privilege of being the obstetrician for one of Kenneth

City of *Faith*, Oral Roberts University School of Medicine

Hagan's granddaughters and Terry Law's (founder of Compassion International Ministries) wife. What a privilege it was for me to be in practice at the COF.

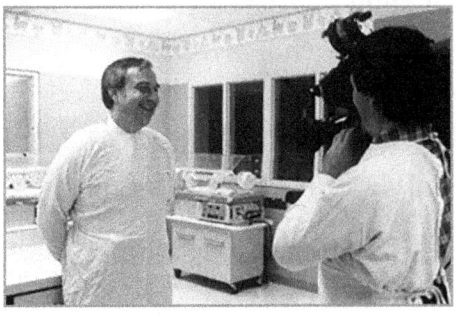

Praying Hands at City of Faith, Hospital and Research Tower.

Dr. Tredway Opening the COF Childbirth Center.

One of the pleasures of working at the COF was the weekly department services we had on Thursday afternoon that was open to staff and patients on a volunteer basis. Others and I would share. I witnessed the staff and physicians mature in the Lord, especially Drs. Mark and Betsy. I will always remember the day that we prayed for and launched them into the mission field when they were called by God to very difficult areas of the world. Betsy was the first obstetrician/gynecologist under my supervision that was called of God to flow in the supernatural. God allowed me to mentor in the ways of Him. I was so blessed to see these two released. While I was disappointed that more opportunities for public ministry did not occur for myself, it took me a number of years to realize that one of my major gifts in God was the releasing of others to minister in the Holy Spirit. I am like a proud papa of these two. Here is a little of Mark and Betsy's story at ORU and the COF.

Drs. Mark and Betsy Neuenschwander: Jesus began His public ministry with the following words: "The Spirit of the Lord is upon Me because He has anointed Me to preach the Gospel to the poor, He has sent Me to proclaim release to the captives, and recovery of sight to the blind, to set free those who are oppressed, and to proclaim the favorable year of the Lord" **(Luke 4:18-19)**. Betsy shares, "I've seen all of this list accomplished in the Name of Jesus from the ministry of Dr. Don and Donna Tredway's lives. Scripture tells us that, **"it is the anointing that breaks the yoke" (Isaiah 10:27).**

I met Dr. Tredway in 1980 when interviewing to be hired as a board-certified Ob-Gyn physician at the ORU School of Medicine where he was Chairman of the Department. My husband Mark, also a physician, and I knew that we had a call on our lives for full-time missions **(Matthew 28:18-20)**. It was wonderful having a boss who was a Ph.D. and M.D. He embodied scientific excellence and manifested the supernatural flow and power of the Holy Spirit. Indeed, we were mentored by the Tredways. We were amazed hearing their exploits which encouraged us to believe that the words of Jesus in **Mark 16:15-18** are still literally true for believers today: "Go into all the world and preach the Gospel. These signs will follow those who believe and preach the Gospel: 'In My Name they will cast out demons, they will speak with new tongues; they will take up serpents, and if they drink any deadly poison, it will not harm them; they will lay hands on the sick, and they will recover.'" Professor Tredway and his wife Donna, who is a nurse, lived these scriptures before us.

In our Ob/Gyn department Dr. Tredway conducted a voluntary teaching/ministry time on Thursday afternoons for staff and medical students. These sessions were anointed manifestations of God's presence and miracles. One of the teachings that deeply impacted me was the power in covenant relationships with that. Don expounded on the covenant that existed between David the warrior and Jonathan, the son of King Saul. After Saul and Jonathan's deaths, King David inquired, "Is there anyone still left of the house of Saul that I could show him kindness for Jonathan's sake?" (**2 Samuel 9:1**). The only survivor was Mephibosheth, a son of Jonathan, who was lame in both feet. Although Saul had repeatedly tried to destroy David many times, now King David called for Mephibosheth, sat him at his own table daily, and restored all the lands and possessions of Saul. This is an example of Jesus with us.

Mark reflects, in his opinion, the anointing of the Holy Spirit grows out of fellowship with God, surrender, obedience, and knowing the authority of scripture. While working as a busy physician, Dr. Tredway's weekday habits included spending time in the early morning being in God's presence in worship and meditating upon the Word (Bible).

In 1986 Dr. Tredway was part of an Apostolic-Prophetic team (as seen in **Acts 13:2-3**) that ministered over us at our commissioning service, launching us into full-time ministry overseas. Don had given us other supernatural words of wisdom to encourage us on prior occasions. That night Don's words would greatly prove to guide, strengthen, and comfort us over the next nineteen years in Asia, including such countries as N. Korea, China, and Afghanistan. For God and God alone!

FOLLOWING THE *Anointing*: PART II

Part of God's mandate on us was to train professionals to use their skill sets strategically and deploy into the most "Unreached Harvest Fields" of the world! God developed through us a "Spiritual Skills" course for professionals, a boot camp training ten days long, ten hours per day. In the early '90s we were so blessed to have Dr. Tredway teach, mentor, and minister in three of these schools on the topics of Divine Healing, Spiritual Warfare, and the Authenticity of God's Word. These sessions were videotaped, taken overseas, and shown in many of our international schools.

We are only two of the people amid the hundreds, maybe thousands, that the Tredways have profoundly touched and influenced. We love them deeply and are forever indebted to them. To God be the Glory!

Don: There are two lessons that I learned during my time of trying to balance ministry and medical practice. One involved the pregnancy of Lindsay Roberts. I had prayed and accepted a FGBMFI regional conference invitation in Columbus from a former medical student from ORU who was in practice in Ohio. Unfortunately, the speaking engagement was during the last month of Lindsay Robert's pregnancy. I informed my friend a few weeks before the event that I could not attend because of this pregnancy. There was also another FGBMFI regional meeting in Modesto, California where I had a conflict with practice again. I asked Mark Neuenschwander to replace me at the last minute for this meeting. The Lord later convicted me that if I had prayed about speaking and had confirmation from Him to accept the invitation to speak, then I should have gone ahead with the engagement. **By not doing so, I was not trusting Him.** This was a hard lesson for me, and I have never been able to ask for forgiveness from those involved. **One needs to be sensitive to the Holy Spirit of how to balance your profession with**

ministry and also with your personal family life. If Paul could do it with his tent making, we can also. Was this again a continual battle with the pride of life?

My time at the COF was one of the most fulfilling times of my life as we observed the Holy Spirit at work in our clinics, obstetrical suites, and operating rooms. Patients would come to the COF who would not go elsewhere because of the spiritual dimension. It was also during this time that I was asked to give my testimony of healing on the Oral Robert's TV program.

1985 was a busy year. I traveled to China again with Dr. Don Dale, his wife, and a group of physicians for another medical teaching trip. Dr. John Coppes was on the trip and spoke on obstetrical topics, and I spoke on Advanced Reproductive Techniques. We toured an Ob/Gyn hospital and had the opportunity to demonstrate by doing a laparoscopy on a patient with endometriosis. (Donna was able to video the procedure.) In preparation for surgery, not only did we scrub our hands but also soaked our hands and arms for five minutes in one hundred percent alcohol. I imagine it would be very hard on the skin if you did many cases in a day.

The trip was almost four weeks long because we also took time for sightseeing. It was quite a trip. We traveled from Hong Kong to Beijing (visited the Great Wall) and on to Tianjin, Qinhuangdao, Yinchuan (the train trip to Yinchuan was twenty-six hours), Xian, Guilin (went on a river trip), and then back to Hong Kong. Yinchuan was a memorable visit because when John and I were walking with a former missionary from Taiwan, we met a couple who had been in the Cultural Revolution, and we were the first people from the West that they had seen in many years. Another significant event in that city was when one evening at a banquet, a Chinese doctor asked why our group didn't drink alcohol. Through that silent witness, I was able to share about Jesus.

It was a beautiful trip. In contrast to my first visit to China, the government was now allowing farmers to sell their products on the street where as before, it was prohibited. Previously we had stayed in a government retreat center for the first week, and the difference between the food we received in the facility and that of the street vendors was quite a contrast. Also, while in Beijing during this trip, I had the opportunity to share on Sunday at the Interdenominational Fellowship.

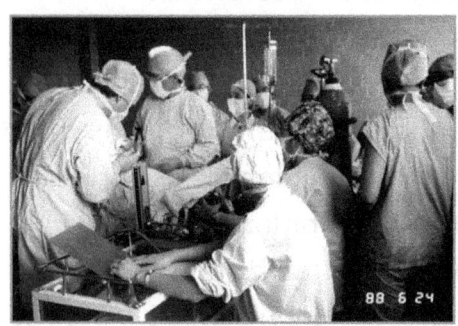

Teaching Laparoscopy in China. Drs. Tredway and Coppes.

Teaching in China with Dr. Dale.

During a teaching engagement at a YWAM Counseling school in Makapala, Hawaii, I received a phone call from Dr. Reginald Klimionok of Garden City Christian Church in Queensland, Australia (one of the largest churches in Australia), asking me to come for a crusade in April 1986. YWAM had introduced him to me at one of their conferences in the area and he asked me to speak in his church on Sunday morning. I accepted the invitation and the Spirit of the Lord fell so strongly that people came spontaneously to the front for salvation and healings without an altar call. Dr. Klimionok was also a friend of Ralph Wilkerson who had shared with him about our ministry. I found that by being an academic physician with an active medical teaching practice from ORU's COF, opportunities were opening for me in public ministry. **Oral's vision of the combination of prayer and medicine was being fulfilled through a marketplace ministry.**

In April 1986 (4-13) Donna and I had quite time in the Lord in Queensland, Australia at Garden City Assembly of God Church. As I have reviewed the old VHS tapes, God released me in words of knowledge, boldness in the Holy Spirit, and major moves of His Spirit. I also was exposed to such profound worship at Garden City that was paramount in releasing the presence of God. After this time, we would develop a friendship with the Klimionoks, whose path we would cross in the future.

CHAPTER 5

Hillcrest Fertility Center
(Persecution and Attack)

    I was soon to be faced with one of the most tremendous challenges of my life. The enemy tried to destroy my reputation as a physician. When I left the University of Oklahoma, I had to leave my association with the Hillcrest Infertility Center. As a reproductive endocrinologist, it was exciting to be involved in the emerging field of assisted reproduction and in vitro fertilization. While at the COF, I tried to form a satellite clinic where we could have the fertility treatments done at the COF and the IVF retrievals at Hillcrest. Unfortunately, the COF attorney and the head of the ethics committee were of Catholic faith and were opposed to fertilization outside of the human body. That was disappointing to me because I believe that God is the source of all knowledge, and as long as we give Him the glory and keep the techniques within the context of the husband and wife, I am at peace. Dean Edwards would not allow me to appeal this decision, so I had to lay aside this part of my practice

FOLLOWING THE *Anointing*: PART II

to which I had been led by the Lord. This was about to change in a dramatic way.

In January 1986 Hillcrest Hospital fired the physician and embryologist for breach of contract for opening another operation at Baptist Hospital in Oklahoma City and for other practices with which they had concern. I had been approached by the hospital administrator advising me of the pending action, and he asked me to take over as director of the infertility center in order to continue care to the patients (I was a Reproductive Endocrinologist and had previously worked at the clinic when I was at OU). I was not able to accept the position since I was an employee of the COF. The administration of Hillcrest went to the COF to talk to the dean, and I was told that I was released to accept the position while continuing my ORU and COF responsibilities.

Then all hell broke loose. Unknown to me, a patient was scheduled for an embryo transfer the day of their firing, and I was called to do the transfer. I had done transfers in the past and explained the procedure to the patient. Another gynecologist colleague from OU, who had been actively working with the fertility center, was also there in order to assist me and even offered to do it. I told him it was better to let me do it in order to protect him from repercussions since he still worked with the physician and embryologist at OU. That was a mistake on my part. When the situation was explained to the patient, she agreed to proceed, but then multiple lawsuits came forth. There were suits and countersuits for eighty-nine million dollars between the hospital and the physician and embryologist as well as a federal racketeering suit against the hospital and me. I was accused of planning to take over the business while I was on the mission field with YWAM, even before returning to Tulsa. In addition, a malpractice suit was filed against me with the claim that

Hillcrest Fertility Center

I was incompetent to do an embryo transfer. Two other malpractice suits were generated against me because of slanderous statements about my medical capabilities by the fired physician. I was one of two board-certified reproductive endocrinologists in Tulsa and still was sued. I couldn't believe it was happening. My relationship with the physician and embryologist deteriorated, and tremendous animosity existed between them and myself in addition to my former staff at OU. I was even being slandered at national meetings, and I had to counter sue to get it stopped. The next few years would be the most difficult years of my professional life. An embryologist from ORU helped me in the embryo culture lab but had a difficult time because the lab employees were loyal to the former embryologist. My office at Hillcrest was broken into, files were taken, and conversations from my home phone were recorded and reported in the plaintiff's court documents. I had four to five lawsuits against me that could potentially destroy me. My name was in the paper, and my children came home and told me what others were saying about me. There is no doubt that an attempt was being made to destroy my identity as a physician and as a witness for the Lord Jesus Christ.

Also, at this time the financial situation at the COF was not good. Medical billing is different than other businesses and one must stay on top of it. As department Chairman I was never able to look at the accounts of the department and had no authority over the billing procedures. The department committed thirty percent of our obstetrical practice to indigent care, which was to be covered by state programs. In order to file the necessary state forms, the patients were to sign the forms while in the hospital, but the billing department would never do it. I had been in major medical centers in California and Chicago where we did efficient billing. I even offered to have a billing company come in and use the Ob/Gyn department as a pilot program to see how it could be done, but to no avail with those in authority. Unfortunately for the COF, the end was in sight. We were not being good stewards of God's resources. My friend Dr. Bruce Thompson from YWAM was asked to come as speaker for a faculty retreat during this time. He prophesized that the COF would close, and its faculty would be disbursed throughout the world. His Word that day was given through the following scriptures. To the faculty:

> **Amos 9:9-11** For behold, I am commanding, And I will shake the house of Israel among all nations As grain is shaken in a sieve, But not a pebble will fall to the ground. All the sinners of My people will die by the sword, Those who say, "The catastrophe will not overtake or confront us."...On that day I will raise up the fallen shelter of David And wall up its gaps; I will also raise up its ruins And rebuild it as in the days of old.

> **Jeremiah 29:14 (AMP)** "I will be found by you," says the LORD, "and I will restore your fortunes and I will [free you and] gather you from all the nations and from all the places where I have driven you," says the LORD, "and I will bring you back to the place from where I sent you into exile."

To the administration and faculty:

> **Jeremiah 23:1-5 (AMP)** "Woe to the shepherds who are causing the sheep of My pasture to perish and are scattering them!" declares the LORD. Therefore, this is what the LORD, the God of Israel says concerning the shepherds who are tending My people: "You have scattered My flock and driven them away, and have not been concerned about them; behold, I am going to call you to account for the evil of your deeds," declares the LORD. "Then I Myself will gather the remnant of My flock out of all the countries where I have driven them, and bring them back to their pasture, and they will be

Hillcrest Fertility Center

fruitful and multiply. I will also raise up shepherds over them and they will tend them; and they will not be afraid any longer, nor be terrified, nor will any be missing," declares the LORD. "Behold, the days are coming," declares the LORD, "When I will raise up for David a righteous Branch; and He will reign as king and act wisely and do justice and righteousness in the land."

During this difficult time at the COF (1986) as noted previously, Mark and Betsy felt that the Lord was leading them to YWAM. This precious couple sensed an overwhelming call to missions and eventually would be used of the Lord in disaster relief and in war-torn areas. This couple was one of the highlights of my time at ORU and the COF. There was no doubt that the Lord had His hand upon them, and I thank the Lord that I was able to be used to pour into their lives. For me, I felt like a proud father as we honored, blessed, anointed, and released them at a special department meeting. I was beginning to see how the Lord would bring young men and women alongside Donna and me in order to help them be released into what God had for them. As I reflect while writing this, I can see how I was used in academic medicine to train and release obstetricians/gynecologists over the years and how God has used me the same way in the spiritual realm – to equip and release men and women into their calling of the Lord. **Often God will just extend our worldly skills into His spiritual skills.**

Because of the frustrations with the financial difficulties at the COF and the amount of time needed to run the Hillcrest Infertility Center (I changed the name to Hillcrest Fertility Center), I resigned my chairmanship position at the COF and the ORU School of Medicine and went full time with Hillcrest in 1987-1988. Dr. Bob Aikman took over the department at COF, and he and the others would stay until it closed. The legal battle with Hillcrest would go on for five years. The hospital provided Pat Kernan as my attorney who was at my side, in and out of court, during those years. Pat was a former football player from Oklahoma State University and army ranger. He was an aggressive attorney and became a close Christian friend. I thank the Lord for providing him in my time of need. My schedule was difficult with depositions and court proceedings, which resulted in me having to work long hours. At the time we were doing between 100-150 IVF cases per year in addition to other infertility and gynecology patients. I eventually hired two other physicians, Dr. Israel Henig and later Dr. Stan Prough, for the Hillcrest Fertility Center to help with the volume of patients. Kitty White, my administrative assistant from COF, joined me as my practice manager since she had experience in medical practice. In addition, Glenda McKinney, with her exuberant personality, would also join us to be our head nurse. I also hired an embryologist, Phil Chan PhD, who would become a life-long friend and important colleague. I enjoyed the practice, but the constant stress was overwhelming at times. We eventually went to court in November 1990, and after three weeks, a mistrial was declared. The CEO of the hospital passed out (had the flu) during a grueling cross examination on the witness stand. A settlement would be finally reached in April 1991, and I would be vindicated from all lawsuits. I am so thankful for all my professional collogues (Drs. Richard Marrs, Charles March, and Howard Jones) who came to my defense during that difficult time.

CHAPTER 6

Ministry During *Turbulent* Times
(Makapala, Hawaii, and Australia FGBMFI Melbourne Convention)

I am thankful that I had my annual teaching for approximately twelve plus years at the YWAM counseling schools in Makapala, Hawaii (northern part of Big Island) during those difficult years of the lawsuits. It was as if I was let out of a closet and God gave me freedom in Him as I ministered. **I have noticed over the years that during the greatest battles of my life, as I would go forth to share His reality, God would not only touch others but would also touch me as I ministered through my weakness.** During the years of legal battles, I recall two situations vividly. One week as I would go into the lecture room at Makapala, the Spirit of God would fill the room as I prayed. I would point to people, and they would be slain in the

FOLLOWING THE *Anointing*: PART II

Spirit and would be out for the whole lecture. Sometimes I would walk by people, and they would pass out in their seats. At times the Holy Spirit would tell me to have individuals stand. I would point my finger at them, and they would be out on the floor for the two-hour lecture sessions. They often would relate how during that time God would speak to them and changed their lives to follow Him. Read Mac's story of his time with the Lord during the schools at Makapala. He would later be used mightily of the Lord in Asia.

Mac Carpenter: I had the privilege of being a student in 1991 when Dr. Don Tredway spoke in the IBC (Introduction to Biblical Counseling) school I was attending at Makapala, Hawaii. Also, he spoke in one school when I served as staff there.

The topic, from what I recall, was ministering in the power of the Holy Spirit; if that was not the topic, it was certainly the ministry that he modeled. Each morning and afternoon, we had different teaching sessions, followed by ministry times. They were corporate sessions where Don, as we called him, would begin to pray for different students. There was always a strong anointing during the times I was there.

The thing that stands out from those times is that the Holy Spirit "knew" what each person needed. The anointing in which Dr. Tredway seemed to walk was a releasing of the Holy Spirit to minister to the heart needs of those present. Sometimes, perhaps many times, Don was not directly aware of what God was doing; he was more the conduit that God used. Those times weren't limited to the "ministry times" either. God, because He loved us, was working within us even in the teaching times. I remember one morning, during a lecture; God asked me if I was willing to give my ministry back to Him. It was not the topic of the morning, but again, there seemed to be a great freedom during Dr. Tredway's week for the Holy Spirit to give or bring what God wanted each individual to receive. For three days, I struggled coming to a place where I could say yes to the Lord. I loved the ministry in which I was involved. During one of the ministry times later that week, I was able to say yes to the Lord. Even though at first it was a bit painful, I am so grateful to God for that challenge. Looking back, I can see that God clearly knew two things that at that time I did not. I genuinely loved the ministry in which I was involved, but that ministry had become my identity. Because the Father loved me, He wanted me to "get" my identity as His son. Laying down that ministry was part of that process. He also had a new direction for me – I didn't realize it at the time – but that was the first step of a new direction for me that has been my focus the last twenty-six years.

I cannot explain it, but through Dr. Tredway's ministry and the anointing in which he walks, there was tremendous freedom for the Holy Spirit to do deep works in our lives. God was doing different things in each of our lives. For some, there was an emotional healing from shame or painful experiences from the past; for others, sometimes Dr. Tredway would pray a prayer that released insight or even an answer to some issue or question that some of my classmates had been asking the Lord about. Other times, the Lord just spoke as He did to me. Sometimes it was intense, but always life giving.

Another takeaway for me from those times is that I recall the peace and joy that would enter our hearts during those times. There is a phenomenon, some call it being slain in the Spirit, but what happens is that you literally fall to the floor. It may sound a bit strange for those who haven't experienced it, but it is actually very gentle. So, often we would literally lie on the floor and enjoy the presence of God during those times.

In His presence, there was such a sense of "feeling light and clean." It makes sense actually when you think about it, as He is a Holy God, and He is love; He is not just loving, but He is love.

> **1 John 4:8** The one who does not love does not know God, for God is love.

Coming into His presence so strongly, it's not surprising that was our experience. Those were blessed times. I heard another man one time refer to ministry times that were similar to what we were experiencing as "the Father's blessing." That seems a really good way to describe what we experienced during those times – the Father's blessing. Jesus said in John 15 that He would send the Helper who comes from the Father, the Spirit of truth who proceeds from the Father. It was as if the Father was just loving on His kids during those times.

The big takeaway for all of us, besides the life-giving and life-changing heart work that God did in so many of us, was that the Holy Spirit is active today and brings comfort and peace to our hearts, as well as confirmation and healing.

Don: Mac has tremendous insight into how the Holy Spirit works. We in the natural want to know everything that is going on, but God will only give us slight understanding. We are called to be ministers, or as Mac says, be **conduits of God's glory**. Isn't it interesting that during this time of trial and struggles in my life that God used me in this way? Not only were others like Mac touched, but I also was encouraged to know that God was with me while I was struggling. I was also empty, but He filled me with His love as He ministered to others. All I had to do was touch, point a finger, lay a hand, and be obedient to what the Holy Spirit was speaking to me, even when I didn't feel like ministering. We are only a vessel. When I am weak, He is strong. **Are you open this day to be a vessel of God glory and to be obedient to follow him and to go through the trials of life purifying who you are in Him?**

During the years of teaching at the YWAM schools in Makapala, I had the opportunity to meet Ron and Judy Smith. They were leaders of the School of Biblical Studies (SBS), which was a year-long inductive study of the entire Bible. They would become dear friends, and they share their experience in what God was doing during these years in Makapala.

Ron and Judy Smith: I suppose the thing that is most striking to me about our times together at Makapala is that we never knew what to expect. I remember one meeting in specific with about 200 people present, and everybody in the room was slain in the Spirit except just two or three of us. Even the worship leader was down. That was pretty amazing. I also remember the times where the Spirit of healing was there so powerfully. I remember one time when you had people in a circle, and you were praying for people's backs, and people were moving in some of the strangest ways; it looked like everybody was using a hula hoop but the hula hoop was invisible. I remember another meeting where you were throwing your jacket on people and everywhere the jacket went people went down. I remember the night we had the meeting by candlelight because all the lights went out. I suppose the thing that strikes me the most is just reflecting back on the holiness of God. Part of God's holiness is his mystery. And I think the thing that always struck me was the mysterious way that God would move, and we never knew really

FOLLOWING THE *Anointing*: PART II

what he was going to do. Judy adds that she basically remembers the same things. Just that the power of God was there.

Don: Most of the meetings that Ron and Judy shared about were the weekly evening meetings that were open to the community. I myself was in awe as I watched God in action. One day after a lecture at Makapala, as usual, I had students come forward for prayer in regard to what the Lord was speaking to them through the lecture. One young man came forward, and as I approached him (I still cannot believe what I did!), I suddenly hit him with my fist in his belly. I hit him hard enough that he fell over. It happened all of a sudden, surprising me so much that I became fearful of what I did. "Oh God, what did I do?" I said to myself. I helped him up, and he essentially said, "Thank you. I needed that." I later learned that he had not passed his former YWAM Disciple Training School (DTS) and this DTS was his second one. In addition, he was sent to the counseling school for ministry. It literally changed his attitude and approach. I don't recommend this approach unless God takes control.

In addition to speaking at the community meetings during the years in Makapala, I would speak in the Counseling Schools and occasionally at a DTS. The leader of the Foundation in Counseling Schools was David De Carvalho, who eventually would become ordained by the Congregational Church and become the pastor of the first Christian church in Hawaii, Mokuaikaua. He also gives insight into what God was doing in student's lives and even his own.

Pastor David De Carvalho: In January of 1981 I met Dr. Don and his wife Donna Tredway in YWAM. Don was a well-accomplished doctor in his field of expertise but now moving in the anointing of the Holy Spirit. He was used by the Lord to lead people into worship and faith for healing.

Ministry During *Turbulent* Times

I had the opportunity to attend and work with biblical counseling schools up in the Makapala retreat center from 1982-1995. During those years Dr. Tredway was a very important part of our ministry as he inspired and led us into so many encounters with God. We witnessed all kinds of miracles. I remember this young family from Canada where the husband had severe back pains. Dr. Tredway prayed for him in one of our public meetings, he began to move his back backward and sideways, and at the end of his moving, he was healed. He went on to continue his work in construction, and every year he volunteers as a mission builder for YWAM in Kona.

During the course of sixteen years, thousands of students were prayed for, and we saw miracle after miracle of people who were touch by the Spirit of God, falling to the ground and receiving a revelation of their Heavenly Father. I also remember a young Hawaiian man who had his foot crushed by a machine at work. After he was prayed for, his foot was healed. It was a serious injury, and they were observing him to see if he would be able to use the foot again. If everything would heal well, the doctors would have to follow with months of therapy. After prayer he was able to return to work. In addition, I remember the time when one of our staff fell down as dead, no vital signs and not breathing. Dr. Tredway rebuked a demonic spirit of death, and she regained consciousness. Students struggling with unbelief and lies from the enemy and showing some mental instabilities were delivered and healed by the power of God.

Forgiveness was an important message Don would bring to us, as people would receive a touch by the Spirit of God, assured that they were loved by God. This made easy for them to forgive and let the offenses go. Many young couples were prayed to have children, resulting in pregnancies with God delivering many children.

The most important part of his ministry was the release of faith and trust on the power of God.

A whole generation was greatly impacted by the power of God throughout the ministry of Dr. Don Tredway and his wife Donna. Even the open-air campaigner ministry from New Zealand, Noel Gibson, was launched in the Holy Spirit with power after the Tredways prayed for him. As a young man, I was greatly blessed by Don and Donna; they encouraged my faith and showed me how to depend on God as my Heavenly Father. Don is one of my heroes here on earth. My life as a missionary and later on as a pastor is a direct fruit of their ministry.

Australia FGBMFI Melbourne Convention

Don: In addition to my annual times in Hawaii, I received an invitation in May 1987 to go back to minister in Australia for two weeks at the national FGBMFI convention in Melbourne, as well as in several other meetings. David Grantham will describe these meetings in Melbourne.

David Grantham: A National Convention of the FGBMFI was held in Melbourne, Victoria at the Camberwell Civic Centre in May 1987. Attendance was around 200 delegates. Dr. Don Tredway was one of the main speakers at the four-day conference. The teaching sessions regarding the gifts of the Spirit and evangelism were excellent. On the final night there was a real presence of the Holy Spirit. As Don was ministering and part-way through his message, he asked everyone in the auditorium to stand and link hands; as they stood, he asked the Holy Spirit to move and minister in the midst in a sovereign way. As he prayed from the stage, the rows of people began to sway and then fall down in the power of the Spirit. There was a real work done in many lives that night with many getting a new infilling and release from various bondages. The auditorium that night was filled with praise and the rejoicing in the presence of the Lord.

Dr. Tredway speaking at FGBMFI, Melbourne, Australia.

Donna with Kangaroos in Australia.

Dr. Tredway FGBMFI, Melbourne, Australia.

Don: During the legal difficulties in Tulsa, the Lord released me to minister in Hawaii and Australia. Through these ministry times, I knew He was with me through these legal trials. **As I was vulnerable to minister out of my weakness, God showed me His love.** All my adult life I had been the consultant, the expert witness, and the one to whom people would come to for advice. While being sued, my opinion had no validity, and I had to rely upon others, especially God, for my defense. God was still dealing with my pride, and I came to understand Paul's comment that, "out of our weakness, He is glorified."

> **2 Corinthians 12:9-10** And He has said to me, "My grace is sufficient for you, for power is perfected in weakness." Most gladly, therefore, I will rather boast about my weaknesses, so that the power of Christ may dwell in me. Therefore, I am well content with weaknesses, with insults, with distresses, with persecutions, with difficulties, for Christ's sake; for when I am weak, then I am strong.

During those years, I am sure that God used these ministry times to boost me up in Him so that I could endure. He also sent precious prayer warriors who would set in the court room and intercede for me while I was faithless.

> **2 Timothy 2:13** If we are faithless, He remains faithful, for He cannot deny Himself.

The more I would minister out of my weakness, the more He would be glorified. As I would share my trials and make myself vulnerable to the audience or individuals, the Holy Spirit would minister in very profound ways to others and to me. Often when I would share, I would receive understanding and revelation.

> **James 5:16** Therefore, confess your sins to one another, and pray for one another so that you may be healed. The effective prayer of a righteous man can accomplish much.

I had a break from the battles in 1988 when Donna and I traveled to China for another medical teaching trip with the Jian Hua Foundation. Dr. John Coppes and his wife also accompanied us. The trip was cut short because the second city that we were to go to was not ready for us and asked us not to come. We took a couple of days in Beijing to sightsee and visit the Great Wall and then went back to Hong Kong. It was a much more relaxed trip. The Chinese people were not as stereotyped by being all dressed alike, and we weren't closely watched. The Tiananmen Square incident was a year later.

CHAPTER 7

Loma Linda University

While all the legal battles were going on in Tulsa, I was approached by the Chairman of the Department of Obstetrics/Gynecology at Loma Linda, Dr. Alan King, (at the urging of the former Dean of ORU, Dean Hinshaw, who had returned to Loma Linda University as President of the Medical Center) to come to Loma Linda and help establish a section of Reproductive Endocrinology and Infertility along with an IVF Center. After much prayer and discussion with Donna, I initially turned down the offer at the end of the year in 1987. I couldn't see how I could leave Tulsa with the legal situation. Afterward, I began wondering if I had missed God by turning down the offer at Loma Linda. 1988 was a very difficult time because of the continual legal battles and depositions.

Later in the year Dr. King (a gynecologic oncologist) was in New York at an oncology meeting. He called and asked if he could stop by Tulsa to visit us. He spent a couple of days with us and invited me again to come and establish the section. They had hired an embryologist, Dr. Johanna Corselli, and had another reproductive endocrinologist from UCLA, Dr. Davidson, in order to start an IVF program. They still wanted me to come and head up the section.

As I prayed, this time I felt the release to go and was thankful for another opportunity. I asked Dr. Chan to come with me as the andrologist and Kitty White as my clinic administrator. I left Tulsa and went to Loma Linda in 1989 with the agreement that I would return to Tulsa for the pending legal trials. I lived in our motor home in a trailer park nearby the university for the first few months while our home was being built in Yucaipa, California. We were unable to sell our home in Tulsa and had it managed by a rental agency. Once again, I was amazed how the Lord had established a relationship with Dean Hinshaw years before in preparation for this move. **If we are obedient and following His anointing, the appropriate doors will open for us.** That said, it is important to be on God's time schedule and not mine, as Donna so often reminds me.

It is interesting to note that the COF would close by September 1989, and the School of Medicine at ORU was suspended by the end of the 1989-90 academic year due to the financial difficulties. Loma Linda University accepted a majority of the ORU medical students in transfer. A few other COF faculty would join the students. I praise the Lord for my time at ORU and the COF. **There is no doubt that this is what the Lord wanted for medicine, the combination of prayer and medicine.** I am so thankful for all my colleagues who came to the COF. They will always have a special place in my heart. My heart cries for whole person medicine as God intended and for the expression of it like it was witnessed during the ORU and COF time. I pray that the Lord will use those displaced physicians, nurses, and healthcare workers from the COF to spread His ministry of healing to the whole person throughout the world.

Loma Linda University

The years at Loma Linda were very fulfilling. Tammy, our oldest, had obtained a commercial arts associate degree in Oklahoma and then did a YWAM DTS in Hong Kong where she met her future husband, and the couple later married in California. Jennifer, second oldest, did a DTS at YWAM Lausanne, Switzerland, went to nursing school at Loma Linda, and also presented us with our first grandchild, Janel. Kimberly, third oldest, did a DTS in Goulburn, Australia, before starting college at King's College in LA. Noel was in high school while I was at Loma Linda. She had finished her freshman year in Oklahoma before we moved, and the transition for her as a teenager was difficult. She was very active in English riding and well established in Oklahoma but had to start all over again in California. She would have challenges in Southern California.

Donna would return to nursing at Loma Linda and worked in post-partum and the nursery. We had a home in the country where Noel and Jennifer had horses on the property. California was more expensive than Oklahoma, so we lived from paycheck to paycheck. I was very welcomed in the department, and we developed a good section and clinic. Dr. Corselli and Dr. Chan directed the IVF and andrology labs. The university built a new clinic and IVF facility for us where we could do oocyte retrievals under conscious sedation and embryo transfers. We had a state-of-the-art andrology lab. Phil Chan developed PCR techniques, and he did pioneer work regarding sperm PCR and the association of HPV with cervical cancer. The oncology unit had multiple tissue slides from cancer cases, and Phil was able to develop techniques to type the HPV from the histological slides, thus correlating with the type of cervical cancer. The IVF lab was successful. God blessed us, and I was invited to Adventist retreats regarding the ethics of advanced reproductive techniques. The university approached these techniques from the standpoint of staying within the Christian context of the marriage between the husband and wife. For me it was a very fulfilling time as a Christian and to be associated with such a university. Infant heart transplants were occurring at that time, and it was a wonderful atmosphere.

Loma Linda Medical Center's Good Samaritan Statues.

Dr. Tredway at Loma Linda Fertility Clinic.

Loma Linda Fertility Clinic Success Celebration.

Loma Linda University

I did return to Tulsa in 1989 to teach at a Spiritual Skills Conference for Drs. Mark and Betsy Neuenschwander. They were developing their own ministry of disaster relief after returning from YWAM and began a yearly, and sometimes biannual, spiritual skills conference from 1989 to 1993 for physicians and healthcare workers. I taught several years for them on spiritual warfare, authority in God, and deliverance. It was exciting to see how they grew in the Lord, had favor, and accomplished major tasks in Him overseas.

While I missed our friends in Tulsa, it was good to start over again and to reconnect with our roots and friends in Southern California. The legal battles in Tulsa continued, but at least it was not an everyday occurrence. I did have to go back to Tulsa for a few weeks in 1990. As mentioned earlier, the head of the hospital passed out under cross examination and a mistrial was declared. The hospital insurance company insisted upon a settlement, and as a condition, the suits against me were dropped; however, there was one settlement to my benefit. I praised the Lord that this stressful time in my life was over. I again understood His lovingkindness and was able to go on to another chapter of my life.

In Southern California I was able to associate with my mentors at the University of Southern California and of course, my spiritual mentor, Pastor Ralph Wilkerson, at Melodyland. Similar to Tulsa and YWAM in Kona, Southern California was a place where the Lord launched me into new areas of ministry. I taught again at the annual Charismatic Conference at Melodyland in August 1990 and received my ministerial ordination for Christian service on August fifth. It was quite an honor for me, but the enemy immediately tried to steal our joy. My son-in-law and his brother had used our Isuzu Trooper SUV the evening of the ordination and had parked it in the hotel

FOLLOWING THE *Anointing*: PART II

parking lot across from Melodyland where we had stayed during the clinic. We had checked out of the hotel, and all of our bags and a briefcase were in the vehicle. Unfortunately, the sliding roof of the vehicle was left partially open, and the car was stolen that evening. When we left the ordination to go to our car, it was nowhere to be found. I spent the rest of the evening filling out a police report. My briefcase in the car had two years of scientific data from which I was writing a scientific paper for publication. The police recovered the vehicle a month later, but we never got the luggage or briefcase back. I lost all the irreplaceable research data. Isn't that just like the enemy, to try to rob one of His accomplishments? Over the years I have come to expect some sort of back lash from the enemy when God moves in my life. But I am here to tell you that Christ is the victor.

Later that year at Melodyland, I did a weekly session on healing for four weeks on Sunday nights. We studied and used the ministry of Jesus as our example. The training of the Holy Spirit during the years gave me an authority and a more in-depth teaching ministry.

In 1991 I had another battle with infirmary. We took our daughter Kimberly to start college at Life Pacific College, which was next to Echo Park in Los Angeles. The school was of the Four-Square Denomination where Reverend Jack Hayford was president. The next year the school moved to the suburbs and changed its name to King's University. Next door to the school was Angelus Temple where Aimee Simple McPherson ministered. I remember walking into the auditorium and sensing the presence of the Lord. The area had deteriorated around the temple, and I really had to trust in the Lord to leave my daughter in that area of LA. We stayed in a nearby hotel, and the next day I had quite a pain in my neck. The pain did not let up, and a day later while on call at night and doing a Caesarian Section with a resident doctor, I noticed I was having difficulty opening and closing my left hand. I contacted the chief neurosurgeon resident and had an MRI scan done of my neck the next day. That night he called me at home and asked me to see him the next day. He informed me that I had three ruptured discs in my neck and that my spinal cord was compressed one-third. He also said it was common ten to fifteen years after a lumbar fusion to have prolapsed discs at higher levels. I found myself in the operating room a few days later having a cervical spinal fusion. I could not believe it happened so fast, yet I had a peace. I had to wear a cervical brace but recovered and was back to work in a couple of months. It was hard for me to believe that I had been used of God in healing and had to have this happen to me. Yet, I knew in my heart that God was in charge and that he was with me.

In the summer of 1992, I again taught at the annual Charismatic Clinic at Melodyland. I had multiple teaching sessions, but one meeting was another significant experience in the Lord. Benny Hinn had had a healing/miracle service one morning in the main sanctuary, which held approximately 2,000 people. It was quite a meeting in typical Benny Hinn fashion. With Benny there was a major move of God with many people being touched, accompanied by wonderful worship and praise. Signs and wonders occurred with demonstrations of God's presence with many people being slain in the Spirit on the platform. Benny would just lift his hand, and people would fall to the ground. His meeting went long after noon, and I was to start my class in the same main sanctuary after lunch at 1 p.m. I must admit I felt very intimated to follow a meeting like that. I could not get a clear sense of what the Lord wanted, which increased my anxiety more. Quite often the Lord will do something like that to me, the professor who likes to be prepared.

FOLLOWING THE *Anointing*: PART II

The Charismatic Clinics usually had someone assigned to lead a short time of praise and worship before each session, and the individual assigned to lead worship did not show up. As Donna will tell you, I have no gift in singing. As I stood up to speak with knees knocking, the Lord came through in a most unusual way. He gave me some words of knowledge, and then His presence filled the sanctuary. People began to spontaneously seek his face. Pastor Kurt Schroeder from Good News Church in Corona came forward after the meeting and noted the contrast between the two meetings. While the power of the Holy Spirit was present in both, the second meeting had the spontaneous presence of God where He drew the people unto Him. Pastor Kurt would become a life-long friend in the Lord, and we would witness major moves of the Lord in his church during the years to come. He and his wife will share their observations in subsequent pages.

The speaking engagement opportunities in Southern California continued along with my work at Loma Linda University. The Reproductive Endocrine Section developed with four full-time physicians including myself, a full reproductive lab, and a research lab, and I was even doing some basic research. I worked with a neurosurgeon who had developed non-invasive clips to put nerves back together with suturing. The clip only involved the sheath of the nerve so that it was not necessary to place suture through the nerve, causing damage itself. I applied this technique to fallopian tubes in an attempt to have less scar tissue from after surgery. I had obtained funds from some phase III drug development studies that I was doing for various pharmaceutical companies and used them as funding for the project. I did successful studies in reproductive uterine horns of rats and reported the results in a major scientific journal.[8] I also presented the results at a scientific meeting as a new surgical application for re-anastomosis of human fallopian tubes for women who had had their fallopian tubes tied for contraception. The technique was not adopted as the advent of IVF proved to have better pregnancy rates. Loma Linda was a wonderful place for me to work in medicine. In addition, the multiple Southern California ministry contacts through Melodyland and the FGBMFI afforded me multiple opportunities for ministry.

One opportunity was to teach at Hope Chapel in Hollywood, California. It was a small church at the time ministering mainly to the homeless in Hollywood. I met the pastor at Melodyland, and he was surprised when I accepted, but I felt the Lord said to go. It was common for the Lord to send me to small early churches. We had a precious time in the Lord and met two young men, Paul and Carl. I will let Paul tell you of his experience.

Paul Klassen: The transformational years of experiencing the glory of God. I first met Don and Donna Tredway when they came to minister at Hope Chapel in Hollywood California. There weren't many people there, maybe around fifty to sixty in the small church, but the presence of God was strong. Don delivered a brief message, although I don't recall the passage he referenced. However, as he began to speak, the anointing of the Spirit grew strong, and when Don started praying for those who desired prayer, it caused some to fall. I was amazed as I had never experienced anything like this. We met during a challenging time for me. Due to several significant setbacks, my friend Carl and I found ourselves homeless.

Several months later, Don and Donna revisited Hope Chapel Hollywood for a weekend of ministry. I had the opportunity to spend time with them, deepening our acquaintance. I remember how Donna accompanied me to a soup kitchen we organized every

FOLLOWING THE *Anointing*: PART II

Sunday to provide meals for the homeless in Hollywood. During this weekend of ministry, the Holy Spirit's presence was palpable, and while I mainly observed, I endeavored to grasp the extraordinary power of God. I was exposed to this new phenomenon during this very challenging chapter of my life. Yet, encountering God in such an extraordinary and powerful way helped me navigate through this phase in my life of being homeless.

Two months later, Donna invited Carl and me to visit them in Yucaipa. Up to that point, I had only witnessed Don and Donna during times of ministry, and naturally I was cautious about where I sat during dinner, fearing that I might accidentally touch Don and also fall under the Spirit's influence. I wanted to ensure that I didn't touch Don, Donna, or anything belonging to them. It was an important lesson for me to realize that they were just regular people, albeit ones through whom God worked miraculously.

About six months later, with Don's and Donna's help, Carl and I moved to Yucaipa, where Don and Donna lived, and joined the church they attended. There, too, Don preached with the same anointing, and periodically, people would be touched by the Spirit, just as they had been at Hope Chapel Hollywood. Don would also get invited to minister at other churches, such as Melodyland in Anaheim. He would drive to the service, and during the service, the power of God would be present. Don would pray for people, and they would fall under the Spirit's influence. Despite speaking softly during his sermons, I remember him saying that all the time he had put in preparing for his sermons would simply be God preparing him to be a vessel for the Holy Spirit.

After a service, when Don finished praying for people, he would try to get to the pastor's office before anyone else stopped him to have a conversation. However, he often didn't make it in time, and I recall seeing him gently guide people away or hold his hands behind his back to avoid accidentally touching them and causing them to fall under the Spirit's influence again. One of the reasons he had me drive him home after the service was that the anointing took a lot out of him, and he would be too exhausted to drive.

A few years later, when I joined YWAM, Don and Donna would be invited to speak for a week-long seminar. Don would minister to the students, and one time, he asked me to lead worship during their visit to Makapala in the north of Hawaii. As I led worship, the Holy Spirit began to move among the people, and powerful things happened. Don would share scripture and pray for people, and people would be overcome by the power of God. Donna would subsequently minister to those who were touched by the Spirit, sometimes praying with them for hours on end.

Personally, witnessing how individuals as highly educated yet ordinary as Don and Donna could usher in the anointing of the Spirit of God was a profound revelation for me. The experiences of traveling, learning, and being touched by the Spirit transformed my life indefinitely.

Those transformational years of experiencing the glory of God, were some of the best years of my life.

Don: Paul and Carl lived with us for a while, and we witnessed their growth in the Lord. However, I had no idea the depth of the Lord's ministry to Paul, as noted above. Over the years Donna would have many people stay in our home, allowing the Lord to move in their lives.

FOLLOWING THE *Anointing*: PART II

Good News Church was a vibrant church under the leadership of Pastor Kurt Schroeder (As I mentioned earlier, Pastor Schroeder had been at the Melodyland service where I followed Benny Hinn). He invited me to speak at his church. He and his wife, Mary Alice, had a dynamic church with multiple associate pastors who were spiritually prepared for a move of God. The congregation of a few hundred had been well taught regarding the gifts of the Spirit and had grasped hold of the Word of God like few congregations I have ministered to over the years. My first engagement there was on a Halloween night, and I spoke on Curses. The congregation responded to the teaching, especially to generational sins, and many obtained significant breakthroughs in their lives. After that evening, the Spirit of God continued to minister nightly in the church, and the outpouring continued for the next several months. God spoke through various invited ministers, including myself, and I was fortunate to be able to speak in many sessions. The Lord had me go through the ministry of Jesus and to do things that He had done. In fact, the Lord spoke to me and asked, **"Are you willing to be a fool for Me?"** For example, He once had me use spit and dirt for healing and deliverance. I was amazed at what God did, and He certainly tore down my academic hang ups. At times I would have a message prepared, and the Holy Spirit would go another way as I stepped onto the platform. Sometimes He would only give me a scripture, and as I read it, His Holy Spirit would manifest and begin to minister. Once he had me read from **Isaiah 6** about putting burning coals to the lips. He had me take a coal (not burning but representative of one) and have people come forward asking the Lord to purify their lips. As people came forward and put their lips to the coal, they were slain in the Spirit, some were delivered, and others healed. Another time the Lord told me to have two associate pastors come forward and act as seraphim before the throne of

God. As people walked between the pastors, the Spirit of God ministered in the same way as mentioned above. The awesome presence of God was apparent, and the meetings would last a long time. **A key to this time was the wonderful worship in the church.** They were a worshiping church led by anointed musicians, and God honored them by manifesting His glory. The Word says that He inhabits the praises of His people.

> **2 Chronicles 5:13-14** ...in unison when the trumpeters and the singers were to make themselves heard with one voice to praise and to glorify the Lord, and when they lifted up their voice accompanied by trumpets and cymbals and instruments of music, and when they praised the Lord saying, "He indeed is good for His lovingkindness is everlasting," then the house, the house of the Lord, was filled with a cloud, so that the priests could not stand to minister because of the cloud, for the glory of the Lord filled the house of God.

Once again, the Holy Spirit taught me the importance of obedience. As I am obedient, His presence will come. **All that I am to do as a minister is to lead people into His presence.** The verse above talks about the importance of worship in bringing about the manifestation of God's, glory. The Corona church was a wonderful worshiping congregation which ushered in the presence of God in such a mighty way. Pastor Schroeder and his wife, Mary Alice, share below their insight into what they witnessed the Lord doing during those meetings in Corona.

Pastor Kurt and Mary Schroeder, 1990 Revival at Good News Church, Corona, CA:

The very first time we met Dr. Tredway was at a Melodyland Conference that occurred in 1990. I believe this conference took place either in August or early fall that year. We had just heard Benny

FOLLOWING THE *Anointing*: PART II

Hinn bring a wonderful word and ministry time, and the service had spilled way over past the lunch hour that had been scheduled.

My husband, Kurt said, "Let's stay on over for the next service. I really feel for the guy who has to follow up after Benny." Dr. Tredway, we found, was a medical doctor who joked about the fact that he was "practicing medicine" and told how he had been healed of a back injury. After hearing his testimony, the power of God became very evident, and the doctor began to minister to those in the service. I think several things struck me that first time meeting about Dr. Tredway:

He was the perfect example of a medical doctor to me. He was soft-spoken, humble, and had a very caring personality, and it was very evident by the manner in which he ministered that he wasn't afraid to wait until the Holy Spirit showed him what to do next. While he was able to move so easily in the Holy Spirit, I'm afraid to say his singing skills were slightly unmusical and sometimes inharmonious sounding. (Sorry doc.) Kurt and I tried to sing a bit louder "Sing Halleluiah to the Lord" in an effort to give him a hand.

We were very fascinated by the how approachable he was. So different than many of the other ministries we had known (and at that time there were many). We asked him if he'd come minister to our congregation in Corona, California. The closest time we could have him come would be Halloween night 1990. He taught on Curses that first night and later on a series teaching on the Miracles of Christ.

Dr. and Donna Tredway would come weekly to our mid-week service and bring us New Testament teachings of Christ's many miracles. We were all so very spiritually hungry and truly, the doctor piqued our interest in seeking Jesus in a manner in which we had never experienced before.

Teaching on the Sprinklings: One Wednesday, we received the teaching on the Sprinklings that occurred in the Bible. Dr. took us to the Old Testament. Not only we were given the Word to hear, but he also gave us the invitation to step out and activate our faith. Any persons needing a touch from God came and lined up in front near the altar area. Several of the pastoral staff would then "sprinkle" water to the person seeking ministry. I will never forget how reticent my husband was to do this. He got a "little water" and sprinkled it on the face of Jeannette Perez. Dr. Tredway told him to put faith in the act and release it once again to Jeannette. This time, Kurt by faith made the gesture of releasing the water with GREAT FAITH! Jeannette fell back under the power of God. Our pride was being exposed, and we were recognizing the fact that as a disciple of Christ, we must follow what our Master is asking of us, even if to us it seems quite humbling and runs the risk of being on public display.

Another Wednesday evening's teachings involved the power of the Holy Spirit to come upon a person in such a degree that even touching clothing could be a conduit for God's touch. The key scripture was found on the story of the woman with the issue of blood (**Matthew 9:20-22, Mark 5:25-34, Luke 8:43**). The fascinating part of the teaching came when he not only gave us the spiritual focus on this healing but also the medical explanation of her illness and its effects upon her entire life.

Dr. Tredway then had us stretch our faith and touch the edge of the suitcoat he wore. I must say that looking back on this teaching so many years later, the key area that was ignited within each of us was that **Jesus could STILL HEAL, and HE CAN STILL TOUCH us**

even thousands of years later. Troy Perry by faith reached out and grabbed hold of the sleeve of Dr. Tredway's jacket, and I saw Troy fly backward as though he'd been launched from a cannon.

Troy's best friend was Dave Barnes. This scene of God's power overwhelming Troy in like manner happened several weeks in a row. Finally, Dave began to poke fun at Troy telling him that he was really beginning to think Troy was making this all up.

The next Wednesday, Dr. Tredway (without knowing Dave's conversation with Troy) called Dave up to grab hold of the edge of his jacket. Instantly, Dave was overwhelmed by the Spirit of God and fell to the ground. He never questioned God's power on Troy again.

Taking it to the Region: We were invited to have a series of meetings at Lake Elsinore First Assembly with Pastor Fred Rodriguez. This is a large church in our area and the meeting was attended by a great many people in the Lake Elsinore area. I will never forget a woman that Dr. Tredway invited to come up and receive prayer. As she came forward to the front of the church, the power of the Holy Spirit fell on her and rather than going "forward" each time she tried to go up – instead, she would "hop" a step back. It was as though there was a collision avoidance system in her that when Dr. Tredway moved forward – she would be supernaturally moved backward. The lady later went to her pastor and was convinced that someone was "pushing" her backward.

Francine's daughter had an eye condition that required laser surgery (retinal atrophy). Dr. Tredway received a word of knowledge, and as she came forward for prayer, Dr. Tredway gave her four prophetic words, "Michelle will be fine." Michelle had a doctor's visit, and the doctor said he couldn't understand why her condition hadn't gotten worse. "There's no reason for you to have laser surgery."

January 2, 1991: This is a journal entry about my little daughter, Jessica Grace, who was six years old at the time: Dr. Donald Tredway ministered at our Wednesday night service in a first of a four-sermon series. Jessica had a baptism of God's Spirit – she had her little hands raised for fifteen minutes straight and waves of glory just filled her. She was slain in the Spirit twice (into my arms). Her Uncle Sil Orozco prayed for her also. Jessica had the most angelic look – priceless!! Renee her sister complained because she wasn't "healed" like Jessica. "I was stuck in the nursery!"

Pastor Mark Schroeder (Kurt Schroeder's brother): One of my most memorable times with Doctor Tredway in his ministry to us during this time was when four of us pastors were being ordained for the ministry. He was invited out with other guest speakers, leaders, and prophets. He came over to me and handed me a Bible and had me put my hands on it. Then he leaned over and whispered two words that have affected my ministry ever since. He leaned over and said, "Believe it." As soon as he said it, I could feel the anointing that comes behind that, and I could sense that every word and every story and every lesson in every revelation was one in which I could believe and trust. I could lean on it as a teacher of the Word of God. One of my greatest moments is when I was ordained for the ministry from a man who with two words affected my life. These forty years that I've been serving the Lord, and I want to thank Doctor Tredway for that.

Don: Even as I write our story, I still rejoice at what I remember God did during those meetings with that small church in Corona. For a number of years, they did an Easter musical pageant at the

FOLLOWING THE *Anointing*: PART II

Corona City Civic Center where many came to a saving grace of the Lord Jesus Christ. The associate pastors and senior pastor went forth from that congregation to form four different churches. What a privilege it was for me to be involved with this small congregation that God blessed with His presence.

While in California, Donna and I planned a two-week vacation in Honolulu at the armed forces hotel, the Hale Koa. Somehow the leadership at the Kona YWAM base became aware that we were going to Honolulu. They contacted me and asked Donna and I to come to Kona for a few days. We accepted the invitation, and when we arrived at the Kona airport we were met and taken to a guest house where we were housed with wonderful hospitality. The next day Donna and I met with two of the base leaders. Quite surprisingly, they asked for our forgiveness. They related that the Lord had convicted them that the base had rejected the ministry of the Holy Spirit in us when we had been on staff. I knew that here was a resistance and never expected anything like an apology. I broke and cried for I did not realize how much I had been hurt. It was a tremendous time of healing for me, and I was so thankful for the leadership in recognizing and acknowledging what had happened.

While in California, I also returned to Tulsa and spoke again for Mark and Betsy Neuenschwander at their Spiritual Skills conference in August of 1993. As I look back, I see how fulfilling the time at Loma Linda was through the ministry times in Southern California, releasing others in ministry and introducing people to the power of the Holy Spirit. The multiple ministries in Tulsa had prepared me for whole person ministry and grounded me in the Word of God. Financially it was difficult at Loma Linda since I was unable to sell our house in Tulsa. We rented it, but it did not pay for all the upkeep and taxes. Jennifer was in nursing school and Kimberly was in college, so I was living from paycheck to paycheck. Every year I would return to Hawaii for a week of teaching at the counseling school at the northern end of the Big Island of Hawaii (Makapala) and occasionally taught at the Kona base.

In 1994 I was getting a stirring in my spirit that there was a change coming. This time when I returned to Makapala, I found that the Counseling School had been moved back to the main base in Kona and that Island Breeze had been transferred to Makapala. I spent time with this group and really prayed about whether I was to return to the main YWAM base in Kona. The head of the counseling and healthcare school at the Kona base had just died and the position was open. I interviewed with David Boyd who was head of the base and also with the person who was head of the academic training programs. Both were encouraging me to return to YWAM. I stayed in my isolated cabin at Makapala and spent time seeking the Lord as to what He would have me do. I received a surprising word. He said that the base did not need a dean but a father. I felt no release to accept the deanship position.

During this time at a nearby local park at Makapala, there was a Saturday festival for slack-key Hawaiian music. There were multiple musicians and lots of food, and I had a wonderful time with the local Hawaiians and Islanders. It was a very relaxing time for me, and I am certain that that is why I enjoy Hawaii so much. I am able to shift into a lower gear and relax. My desire was always to spend part of the year in Hawaii and the rest of the year on the mainland. It did not seem possible at the time but at least with YWAM, I was able to go every year and teach. Unfortunately, Donna did not accompany me most of the time. She had returned to nursing, working at the Loma Linda University Hospital.

FOLLOWING THE *Anointing*: PART II

I was very busy with my medical practice at Loma Linda and with speaking engagements at various churches on the weekend. We became involved with a local charismatic church, Rock Church, in the San Bernardino area, which started from a small Bible group of twelve people meeting at a local motel on Sunday. The founding pastors were Jim and Debbie Cobrae. The church grew to a few hundred people while we were there and is now one of the largest churches in the that area – The Rock Church and World Outreach Center.

Jim, at one time, was also a contractor, and I met him when I was looking for a place to live. He had built a new home for sale in Yucaipa that was thirty minutes from the Loma Linda Medical Center. We bought the house, came to know the Cobrae's, and became involved in the early days of the church. Jim's messages were from the Word of God, precept upon precept. His teachings continued to build on the platform and experiences from Tulsa, especially on the teachings of Bob Yandian. This became our home church, and I had opportunities to share and minister there and saw the Lord move through signs and wonders.

The section of reproductive endocrinology continued to grow, and I was elected by the staff to the OB/GYN department's executive board. A Seventh-day Adventist physician who had completed a fellowship at UCLA, Dr. Samuel Pang, and a Loma Linda resident who had done a fellowship in reproductive endocrinology at University of Georgia, Dr. Yvonne Whitney (later to become Dr. Carol Peters-Tanksley), joined our section's staff. It was a dynamic program, and there were multiple opportunities to share and pray with patients. It is interesting to note that after my leaving Loma Linda, Dr. Carol's and my path would cross again. She would eventually go to ORU to complete a Doctorate in Ministry.

Loma Linda University

Dr. Carol Peters-Tanksley: Dr. Donald Tredway was my first boss and mentor after completing medical training. I was young and not very wise. His leadership and example as a physician made a huge impression on me. Because of that he will always be "Dr. Tredway" to me. And that would be enough.

But that's not what I think of when I think of Dr. Tredway. Instead, I think of transformation – my own, and his. I think of what God can do with someone when He is given the opportunity.

The last time I saw Dr. Tredway in person, over twenty-five years ago, he gave me a book. Although I'm sure he knew I needed it, he had no idea how badly. Only later, when I was experiencing the darkest days in my own journey, I finally pulled out that book and read it. Beyond all the other help I received or material I read, that book was God's lifeline for me. It, and the memory of Dr. Tredway, became a critical catalyst in bringing me out of darkness and into His glorious light.

But to see Dr. Tredway's own transformation has been truly inspiring since we have connected again. I don't know all the steps God used to break and rebuild him; I do see the results. He has left all hiding behind and made the whole of himself available for God to do with as He will. As important as his scientific/medical contributions were, his character has become what God has used to make a difference in the last many years through ministry around the world. The Holy Spirit has become his closest companion and deepest joy. And how many thousands of people God has transformed as a result of Dr. Tredway's being available only eternity will show.

The anonymous poet who penned "When God Wants to Drill a Man" could have been writing of Dr. Donald Tredway.

FOLLOWING THE *Anointing*: PART II

> "How He bends but never breaks
> When his good He undertakes;
> How He uses whom He chooses,
> And which every purpose fuses him;
> By every act induces him
> To try His splendor out-
> God knows what He's about."
>
> —Anonymous

Don: The book that I gave Dr. Carol was *This Present Darkness*, by Frank Peretti.[9] Many of us are blind to the spiritual world until the Holy Spirit opens our eyes. The book was also an eye-opener for me in my spiritual walk. Dr. Carol shared more in the chapter on "Inner Healing" and in the section on "Shame" in Part I of our journey.[1]

The OB/GYN department at Loma Linda also had a very strong oncology unit in addition to gynecology, perinatology, and my section of reproductive endocrinology and infertility. Three different hospitals were used for training (Loma Linda University, San Bernardino County Hospital, and Riverside County Hospital), and the combination of those hospitals offered excellent training for students and physicians. The faculty was based at all three hospitals with some of the budget coming from the county hospitals. I was fully based at the university hospital although I did have a weekly infertility clinic at Riverside County Hospital. The relationship between the University Department of Obstetrics and Gynecology and the individual county hospitals was based upon contracts that came up for review every few years. During my time at Loma Linda, there developed a strained relationship between San Bernardino County Hospital and our department chairman. It deteriorated to the point that it looked like our department was going to lose its contract. Since a loss could affect other departments, the president of the Loma Linda University Medical Center, Dr. Hinshaw, called me into his office and asked me to be his negotiator for the department of OB/Gyn and San Bernardino County. The contract was critical for the University. My chairman was informed so I assumed the role. There were several meetings with our faculty and the San Bernardino County, and I was able to negotiate a suitable contract. Nothing was ever said, but that experience seemed to have strained my relationship with the chairman. There were other episodes in which conflicts arose between the chairman and other hospitals. Both the dean of the medical school and the president of the medical center advised me that they thought they were going to have to replace the chairman and asked if I would be willing to take over the department. I was shocked and the question reminded me of my struggles in Tulsa at the Fertility Center. I responded that as long as he was chairman, I would be loyal to him. If they decided to remove him, then I would be open to being interim chairman and a candidate for the position that would then be determined by the usual search committee. To this day, I am not sure if the chairman was aware of these conversations, but our relationship seemed strained after that. I did sense that there was some political infighting occurring at the university.

I had no idea what God was going to open up for me in our next journey with Him. I received a letter from a recruiting firm looking for a Chairman of the Department of Obstetrics and Gynecology at King Fahd National Guard Hospital in Riyadh, Saudi Arabia. I discarded the letter, but something made me pick it up and take it home to share with Donna. The letter explained that they were looking for Western academicians to come and help them convert from a British to a North American-type training program in order to obtain hospital accreditation with the Joint Commission

FOLLOWING THE *Anointing*: PART II

Accreditation (JCAH) of the US. I am not sure how they got my name, but I shared with Donna, and she was open to the possibility. I prayed about it for a couple of weeks, and the idea just wouldn't leave my mind. It is funny how God puts things together. During the time of seeking the Lord for direction, I then had a patient from Saudi Arabia whose husband was a colonel in the Saudi Army. I asked about the hospital, and he encouraged me to go, so I finally contacted the recruiting agency which was in Canada. With my academic and Navy background, I was asked to apply, and they offered to send me on a site visit to check it out. Both Donna and I had a peace about exploring the possibility, so I advised the recruiting agency that I would like to visit the facility in order to evaluate the position. My prayer then was for the Lord to close the door if this was not where we were to go. I had also been praying about returning to YWAM.

They sent me a one-way first-class airline ticket to Riyadh, Saudi Arabia. I flew to New York, transferred to Swiss Air, and landed in Riyadh late at night where a representative from the hospital picked me up. He took me to the housing section of the hospital compound and showed me where to pick up the compound bus in the morning for my interviews. I was tired but excited as I went to bed in a furnished apartment similar to what we would be provided if I accepted the position. The next morning, I took the bus to the recruiting agency's office where I had various interviews with the Canadian medical director, a US hospital administrator, and various department chairmen from different countries. The acting chairman of Obstetrics and Gynecology was a Sudanese doctor. He was very friendly and introduced me to the physician staff of twelve, male and female. There were also an equal number of doctors in training, registrars (residents in US terms), all female except for one male, and all were of Arabic descent – Egyptian, Palestinian, Lebanese, Syrian, Saudi, and US. It was a very busy obstetrical service with 500 deliveries per month. The female doctors in training wore veils so all I could see of their faces were their eyes. Fortunately, the female staff did not have to wear them. One of the resident doctors had been in training for twelve years and could not pass his qualifying exams.

I now realize that I am a builder, and I like new challenges. My time at King Fahd Hospital certainly was a challenge. I sometimes regret not staying at the same place for longer times in order to develop continuity and longevity, but that is not my nature. I was intrigued by the environment and saw another adventure before me. As I prayed on the way home (yes, they gave me a return ticket home), I felt the Lord had opened this opportunity for me. Donna agreed and we made plans to leave. All of our girls were all on their own, so it was just the two of us at home. I talked to the chairman and asked for a two-year leave of absence to which he agreed. I accepted the position at the King Fahd National Guard Hospital and was offered a five-year contract. We sold our house, and I went ahead of Donna to Riyad. I had been at Loma Linda for five years (1989-1994).

CHAPTER 8

Saudia Arabia
(True Desert Experience)

King Fahd Hospital was a military hospital for the Saudi's National Guard and was under the direction of the Crown Prince, Prince Abdullah. The king at the time was King Fahd whose royal hospital was King Faisal Hospital. Riyadh had other hospitals as well, military, public and private. The previous chairman of OB/GYN at King Fahd had been a perinatologist, and the hospital had had a recent change in the Saudi Director. The Crown Prince appointed the former director of King Faisal Hospital, Dr. Jabar, to King Fahd Hospital in order to reorganize and update it. He was a very intense and in no uncertain terms told me that he wanted an updated department and advised me not to depend too much on the current staff. I shared with him that we needed an improved obstetrical delivery unit, and I wanted to establish a high-risk obstetrics division, an oncology division, an IVF program, and a midwife service. He encouraged me, as did the medical director and administrator of the hospital. The next few months were spent building relationships with my attending staff, residents, fellow chairmen,

FOLLOWING THE *Anointing*: PART II

and nursing and hospital staff. I was able to recruit a head OB nurse from Dallas, Texas, whose husband was in the US military. She came from Parkland Hospital where she had the experience from a high-volume obstetrical service. We were also able to establish a midwife service and hire a perinatologist (high risk obstetrics) and an oncologist. In addition, we reconfigured the obstetrics unit by adding a larger triage area through utilizing my staff's office space that was located in the prime patient care area. Not all staff appreciated their offices being displaced, but we were able to relocate staff offices to an outlining area of the hospital. Those on call for obstetrics were still in the delivery area. We accomplished all of this in the first year. I was mainly an administrator, although I introduced teaching rounds every morning at morning report, weekly chairman rounds where residents would present patient cases, and operative gynecologic laparoscopy.

The last area to be developed was the area of reproductive endocrinology and infertility. At the end of the first year, Dr. Jabar called me into his office and advised me that he had hired a Dutch reproductive endocrinologist to begin the section and set up an IVF program. That was quite a surprise to me as I had been ordering the equipment to set up the section to start it. I was disappointed because I would not have the opportunity to practice my area of expertise and that was contrary to the understanding that I had when hired. The doctor came and was gracious and established an independent unit separate from the department.

The department grew with the different subspecialties. Through the support of different drug companies, I introduced operative laparoscopy and set up the first operative laparoscopy course in the country. In the US we usually practiced on pigs, but that was not an option in Saudi. We used goats. I had no trouble getting the anesthesiologists to help since their pay was taking home the goats after they were sacrificed at the end of the procedures. The course was very successful and popular with gynecologists attending from all over the country. The course was run through the continuing education department of the hospital. After the success and popularity of the course was evident, I was advised by the head of the continuing education department that in the future the director of that department would be running the program and not me. This was a common practice of the Saudis. If something was successful, the Saudi director would take the program over. That decision did not bother me because I was hired to raise up the training program so that the local doctors could take over.

After two years at King Fahd, Dr. Jabar, the person in charge of the National Guard medical programs, called me into his office and offered me the position of medical director of the National Guard Hospital in Jeddah, Saudi Arabia. He presented it as a promotion and advised me that the Dutch IVF doctor would take over the OB/GYN department. That was a sudden and unexpected surprise, so Donna and I flew to Jeddah and spent a weekend evaluating the situation. I interviewed with different staff people at the hospital while Donna looked at the housing and local situation. I wondered if the Lord was opening another door for us. It would mean that I would have to leave my current clinical situation and become a full-time administrator as well as leaving established friendships and the underground Christian community. We did not have peace, and I declined the offer. It was beginning to look like our time in the Middle East was becoming short.

Donna had arrived in Saudi Arabia a month after me and worked as a nurse in the diabetic clinic. There were no Saudi nurses since the women by tradition stay in the house, so all of the nurses were

FOLLOWING THE *Anointing*: PART II

expatriates mainly from the Philippines. Some were also from Egypt along with a few from the West. We lived in hospital accommodations on the hospital compound and became close friends with the head of nursing and her husband from the US and with a male nurse and his wife from England. Both couples had been working in the country for several years and would take Donna and I out to show us the "lay of the land." They would also take us out into the desert where we would find ancient seashells and articles from the times when the land was covered by an ocean. We enjoyed exploring the area, visiting the never-ending shops in town, and trying to understand the culture. We also enjoyed guided trips within Saudi to places that one would ever see except through those offered by the hospital. In our travels we saw evidence of old Jewish populations and early Christian churches. Over the course of time, evidence of these places had mostly been destroyed.

The traditions and customs of the country were difficult as a Westerner to get used to. Bartering was a way of life when it came to purchasing anything from Persian rugs to jewelry to small items sold by the homeless widows on the street. The Mattawa, the religious police, were especially on the lookout for Westerners, especially women, to make sure that they were properly covered with the headgear, long sleeves, and skirts that were proper length below the knees (no elbows or ankles were to be seen, and the hair was to be covered). If there was a transgression, the husband would be told to correct his wife. Donna was even tapped on a shoulder with a camel prod by a Mattawa who told her to cover her head when her scarf had slipped down. We also had to carry an Arabic translation of our marriage license with us to prove that we were married. Women were not allowed to walk alongside of or with a man unless it was her husband. They were also not allowed to walk in public by themselves. They always were made to walk in groups.

The weekends in Saudi were Thursday and Friday and for us, that was quite an adjustment to make. Then there were the five calls to prayer that rang out all over the city calling the Muslims to pray. Stores would close, and the streets would clear of people, or the Mattawa would gather them up and take them off – where to, I don't know. Thursdays were also the days that Westerners were warned not to go shopping, especially around the area of what was known as "Chop Chop Square," the place of public punishments and executions. The Mattawa were known to gather Westerners and make them watch the carrying out of the punishment.

The desert heat was also a factor in making our adjustment. Shopping was done in the morning or evening as most shops closed in the afternoon because of the heat. Temperatures would climb well above 120°F during the summer. Hydration was always a necessity and so was air-conditioning.

The month of Ramadan was another interesting event to get used to. There was no eating or drinking from sunrise to sunset, but as soon as the sun was down, there was great feasting. During the day, even the water fountains in the hospital were covered so that no one could drink.

Our time in Saudi was truly a desert time, especially spiritually. We were not allowed to bring in Bibles or any other Christian literature and were absolutely forbidden to wear any kind of jewelry, such as a cross, that represented Christianity. There was no understanding of the love of God. For the Muslim, God was seen as belligerent and legalistic, and their relationship with Him was based on following the Koran and obedience through works.

FOLLOWING THE *Anointing*: PART II

It took a year until we found an underground church. One had to be careful who you talked to when trying to explore "are you a Christian?" You certainly didn't want to be turned into the military police. Somehow, we learned that there were church services at the British Embassy and from there learned of services held on the American military base. Because I was former military, I was able to join an officer's type club, found Christian fellowship, and began attending church services on the base. On one of our Easters in Saudi, I was able to give the sunrise service message. What a privilege.

During our time in Saudi, there was no internet, no fax, and only limited telephone service. There were no more annual trips to YWAM, and all my contacts with the organization disappeared as younger leadership took over. Ministry wise, it was a very dry time. I remembered the devotional, *Streams in the Desert* by Lettie Cowman.[10] Instead of reading the devotional, I was living it.

The senior staff at the hospital was given the opportunity to move to a new Western compound that was very much like what you would find in Arizona or Southern California. It had a large pool with a wave machine and other major amenities such as a bowling alley. We moved and there met expatriates from many parts of the world whose jobs were diversified – everything from bankers to defense workers. We met other Christians there and had monthly Bible studies at our various homes (potluck dinners, to outsiders).

All around us was Islam. I witnessed legalism to an extreme, and through that exposure, I came to a new understanding of the grace of God. The hospitality of individual Arabs was wonderful. We found them to be very gracious and had good times as a couple with our Saudi friends and fellow Arab workers. If we met with them in

Saudia Arabia

a group setting, however, the men and women were separated into different rooms as there was to be no mingling of men and women together. While living in Saudi was an experience of many extremes and challenges, we missed our family. Fortunately, at the expense of the hospital, we were able to fly home and return first class for a two-week vacation yearly. It was always hard emotionally for Donna to return as life there is very restrictive and difficult for women. We could spiritually feel the oppression when we hit the Saudi airspace. It didn't help, either, knowing that when one returned, your passport would have to be turned in and held by the employer. In planning to leave Saudi, one had to apply six weeks ahead of time for an exit and entry visa before getting your passport back. You were at the mercy of your employer. Also, I was still in the military reserve, and once a month I would go to the US Navy base Bahrain to work for a weekend.

Our third oldest daughter, Kimberly, graduated from Biola College in Southern California and wanted to visit us in Saudi Arabia. It was quite an ordeal just to get permission for her to go. On a return trip to Los Angeles, the two of us had to go to the Saudi Embassy in Los Angles and interview in order for her to get a visa. They had to know that I was her father and was giving my permission. Kimberly eventually came to Saudi and was a free spirit who did not like to wear a scarf over her head. I was certain that we would be stopped by the religious police while she was there, but we made it through the visit. She had a wonderful time shopping and spending time with us, but I must admit, I was relieved when she returned home.

As previously stated, Saudi was truly a desert experience for me. I would have liked to have been able to pray for patients and see the release of the Holy Spirit to heal and set people free. I know

FOLLOWING THE *Anointing*: PART II

the importance of signs and wonders and seeing the reality of Jesus Christ established. Instead, I felt bound in chains and surrounded by oppression. There was no understanding of the love of God or of being a son and daughter of the King. My heart cries for the Islamic people who live in in bondage not understanding the love of God or having the revelation of God as a father, Jesus as a friend, or the Holy Spirit[1] who equips. (Some of my Muslim collages told me I would make a good Muslim and even offered me a Koran.)

After our second year in the country, the radical Muslim element became more apparent. Pipe bombs were found in our local grocery store. Our compound became protected by armed guards, and concrete barriers were placed at the entrances. There were also high concrete walls around the compound. The atmosphere at the hospital was also becoming uncomfortable. Rumor had it that I was a Catholic missionary, which my Western friends discounted since they knew I was not of the Catholic faith. I started receiving phone calls at my residence asking what one had to do to be saved and could hear the clicking of a recorder in the background. It was apparent that our time in Saudi Arabia was ending, and I found it difficult going to work. I lost my joy and sensed a change was coming.

I wrote letters to my chairman at Loma Linda advising him of the situation and my desire to return from my leave of absence. He never responded, and it was apparent that there was no place for me to return at Loma Linda. I was very disappointed and prayed, "Lord, what now?"

I received an invitation to fly to Philadelphia to interview for a job with a major pharmaceutical company. At that time, I was due to fly for a medical meeting in the States. So, I stopped by Philadelphia to interview, which happened to be during a major snowstorm. What

Saudia Arabia

a contrast to the desert of Saudi Arabia. The job did not materialize, but I had also received an invitation go to Kansa City to take over a practice and set up an IVF center for IntegraMed America, a US subsidiary of an IVF group in Australia. I had a successful interview for the position and then approached Dr. Jabar about leaving King Fahad Hospital and was released from my five-year contract from the National Guard. Donna left for Oklahoma a couple of months before I returned. I arranged for shipment of our household goods and left after two and a half years. Upon our return to the US, we learned that there had been a change in leadership at YWAM in Kona, and my contacts were no longer there, and there was no opportunity to return to teach. We would continue to have decreased opportunities for ministry during the next few years.

CHAPTER 9

Kansas City and Return to Tulsa

We moved to Kansas City and would be there for the next year from 1996 to 1997. IntegraMed had taken over a private reproductive endocrine practice in Kansas City from an African American physician, who had left to go to Meharry Medical College as Chairman of the Department of Obstetrics and Gynecology. He had left the practice a couple of years prior but would return for a weekend once a month to see patients. A nurse practitioner managed his patients during his absence. I was hired to establish a new office and an IVF service and to take over the practice after a year. The embryologist was from IntegraMed of the Chicago area and would come when we had IVF cases in order to supervise the IVF technician who also did the andrology work for the center. Peter Callan of IntegraMed was the regional administrator, and Gayla Andriano was the Kansas City office manager. We had a beautiful brand-new office on the Plaza in Kansas City with state-of-the-art material. The embryology lab was located in the facility, so egg retrievals were done in the office. It was exciting when our first IVF patient became pregnant since the pregnancy rate was only around six to ten percent in those early days of IVF.

Gayla and I went to various practices in the area in an attempt to build up a referral practice. I enjoyed the practice, but it was a lot of work to reestablish it. In the office I worked with the nurse practitioner, and for operative gynecologic procedures I used St. Luke's Medical Center and Research Medical Center in Kansas City, Missouri. It was also quite a change for me to operate by myself in surgery. I missed teaching students and residents.

Kansas City was certainly a welcome change after the Middle East. We bought an old English Tudor home on Ward Parkway in Kansas City that was full of charm and built during prohibition. We also found a wonderful church, Full Faith Church of Love, in Shawnee Mission, Kansas. How good it felt to be free and to openly express our Christian faith. I will never forget the first Sunday when we heard someone say "praise the Lord" out loud in church. Both Donna and I shifted in our seats because we had become so conditioned and fearful in Saudi Arabia, not outwardly expressing ourselves as Christians. The church was very mission-oriented, and through it we found a YWAM connect. Dean Sherman from YWAM Kona was a frequent speaker at the church. We even hosted a YWAM group from Tyler, Texas in our home.

We did return to Kona for a visit in 1996. David De Carvalho, who had been leading the counseling schools in Makapala, had stepped down and was now the pastor of the Kohala Congregational Church in northern part of the island of Hawaii. We visited with him and his family, and I had the opportunity to speak one Sunday at his church. It was good to minister again and felt as if God had let me out of a closet for a brief time. We had very little contact with the

Kansas City and Return to *Tulsa*

YWAM base as we did not know the leadership and they didn't know us. Was our time with YWAM at an end?

Back in Kansas City, the time went by fast, but it was a struggle financially. We lived from paycheck to paycheck, and our savings dwindled. I had accepted a lower salary in order to return to the US and anticipated an increase after the first year when the practice was more established. The physician changed his mind and decided to return to Kansas City after a year and stepped down from the Meharry Medical School Chairmanship. There was only enough business for one physician, and in order for me to remain, I would have no increased salary and would have to assume approximately fifty thousand of debt for the practice. I was not comfortable to assume this debt and declined. For the first time in my life, the office manager, Gayla, informed me that I was fired. The practice could not sustain two physicians and a nurse practitioner. I could not believe it; I had never been fired in my life, and it shook me to the core. In fact, the shoe was usually on the other foot for I was the one who would be in authority to fire people. I was given my last paycheck and was there with no job. In addition, my contract would not allow me to remain in the Kansas City area to practice because of a one year non-compete clause. I called Tulsa and talked to my former colleague, Dr. Prough, at my old practice at Hillcrest Infertility Center. I was really downcast, depressed, and prayed that God would open doors for us. One week after I was fired, the medical director of Hillcrest Hospital called me and asked me to return, offering me a position. One week after being fired, God opened the door for me to return to Tulsa in 1997 after being in Kansas City only one year.

We had sold our Tulsa house after returning to Kansa City. Donna never thought it was right for us to do, but my accountant said it was

FOLLOWING THE *Anointing*: PART II

good for taxes since we had lost so much over the years while we were at Loma Linda and in Saudi Arabia. I listened to the accountant and at my insistence, sold it. Consequently, we had no house to return. I had bought 120 acres of ranch land in Broken Arrow, a suburb of Tulsa, while we were in Saudi Arabia. There was an old farmhouse on the property in which we let our youngest daughter, Noel, and husband live. We had just enough money to buy a fifth wheel trailer, and for the next couple of years, Donna and I lived in it. All of our savings were gone from living in Kansas City, and we were broke even after the sale of the Kansas City house. We put our furniture in storage and parked the trailer in Noel's driveway. We would like to have bought a house, but there was no way until I become more financially stable. I was shocked by how financially good the physicians had done in the practice I saved during the turbulent times. I was now the junior partner in a practice where a few years earlier I had been the senior partner. It was a difficult pill to swallow, and I had a "pity party." I said, "Lord, look how I have served you. I'm not seeking riches, but now I have nothing while others do." This was a down time for me.

A prophetic friend of ours from our days at Melodyland, Dick Mills, came to town to speak at a local church. He called us and wanted to meet for breakfast. We met him, and he wanted to know what we had done since Melodyland. As we brought him up to date, he pulled out a piece of paper and gave us multiple prophetic scriptures which essentially said, "go build a house." I was blown away. With no money, we started looking at house plans and were introduced to a builder who showed us his home that he had just built for himself. It was a perfect house for us, a one-level three-bedroom brick home. We had him look at our property and in faith signed a contract with him. I then had to secure financing. With no savings

Kansas City and Return to *Tulsa*

or down payment, only on the basis of a Word of the Lord given by our friend, I approached a local bank for a construction loan and another bank for a subsequent permanent loan. We went through the appraisal process, and the land had appreciated so much in value that it was the collateral that we needed to obtain a loan. **What a good God we serve. He goes ahead of us and prepares the way when we do not even know it.** This all happened when I was not active in ministry.

One of the reasons God took me to Saudi Arabia was to see a society that does not comprehend His love. How He wants us to know that life changing love and wants that love to manifest in our lives.

I kept remembering what He told me upon my return to medicine, **"Not one person has to be healed or saved through you for you to be loved by me."** How hard it was for me to come to that understanding.

> **1 Corinthians 13:1-2** If I speak with the tongues of men and of angels, but do not have love, I have become a noisy gong or a clanging cymbal. If I have the gift of prophecy and know all mysteries and all knowledge; and if I have all faith, so as to remove mountains, but do not have love, I am nothing.

Do you know His love, or are you like me that for so many years tried to earn God's love through works? Did the Lord take us to Saudi Arabia away from active ministry so I would come to know Him and His love? Jesus came to take us home to the Father, and all we have to do is surrender to Him and accept Him as our savior. I did not earn it. Is He the love of your life and do you feel His love and acceptance?

It was good to return to Grace Church and the teaching of Bob Yandian.[2] The anointing that he has to expound upon the Word of

FOLLOWING THE *Anointing*: PART II

God is profound. It was wonderful to sit under that anointing and bask in the presence of the Holy Spirit. I found, too, that most of my colleagues from ORU and the COF had stayed in the Tulsa area and were working in various hospitals in the area, and because of their presence and influence, prayer became accepted more openly in the Tulsa hospitals. Dr. John Crouch had taken the family medicine program from ORU to establish a nationally recognized program, In His Image, in affiliation with Hillcrest Hospital and eventually with St. John Hospital. The program with ministry to the whole person had blossomed, and an outreach to the underserved in the community and overseas missions were established. The vision that we had at ORU was being fulfilled. The Family Practice program was the only program to continue the medical ministry of ORU. God kept Oral's vision of the combination of prayer and medicine in spite of man closing the COF. Praise His name!

Our house was finally built, and we moved into what was to become our retirement home on a one-hundred-and-twenty-acre ranch in Broken Arrow. We put up fencing and ran electric fence around the unused portion of land and then leased the land to our neighbor for cattle and hay.

The ranch was therapeutic for me. I would spend the evenings or weekends working on fencing, barns, and general upkeep which never stopped. It was so different from my days at the office in medicine, and it was good to be active and work outside. It was also good to be involved again with the family, and we gave each daughter five acres. Noel and her family lived in the original farmhouse, and our oldest daughter Tammy built a home on the property. Jennifer was in the Navy out of the area, and Kimberly married and was living in the Los Angeles area.

Kansas City and Return to Tulsa

In 1998 the Lord opened opportunities for me to speak at various Korean fellowships in Southern California. Our daughter Kimberly and her husband lived in the area and accompanied Donna and me as we ministered at a Korean church in Ontario. I had asked Jon (her husband) to help catch people if they fell under the power of the Holy Spirit while we prayed for them. There was a wonderful move of the Spirit that ministered deeply. Kim relates the impression of that service.

Kim: The Holy Spirit was moving greatly, people were falling down in waves, and Jon had never seen anything like it. I think his eyes popped out of his head at one time.

Don: Once again as the Lord demonstrated His power, more of the congregation came forward seeking His presence. **How God continues to use signs and wonders to draw people unto Himself.**

The time in Tulsa was one of re-establishing our home. Two daughters were already living there and the other two would eventually return. It was also good to be back in my area of reproductive endocrinology and not to be in charge. There were three physicians and one embryologist, and the practice was doing good. Old patients began to return and, in some cases, a second generation. I was busy. One afternoon I started having chest pain, and when I went to see my internal medicine doctor, he hospitalized me. The next morning, I had a cardiac catheterization and once again recalled my father dying at age fifty-two and two uncles in their '50s. The catheterization was normal, and I was diagnosed with gastric reflex and started on treatment.

But then another medical challenge occurred not with me but with Donna. She was being treated for high blood pressure (BP), but her BP was hard to control. She would have spells where her BP

FOLLOWING THE *Anointing*: PART II

would be 220/140 or more. She was visiting our daughter Jennifer who was a Navy nurse stationed at Camp Pendleton in California and had a spike in BP while driving that resulted in her being taken to emergency room of the Naval Hospital.

When she returned home, she had more workup for the hypertension that had become difficult to treatment by multiple medications. In October 1999, she had a nephrology consultation and a renal arteriogram which confirmed bilateral renal artery stenosis subsequently found to be secondary to fibromuscular dysplasia. For it to appear in both kidneys was most unusual. I was in the X-ray department watching the angiogram procedure that was being done by a radiologist friend. It was evening. Donna had been waiting all day for the procedure to be done. I remember Donna asking my colleague if he was too tired to do the procedure after a long day, to which he replied that he was fine. We proceeded and did a successful angioplasty of the left renal artery, but when he attempted angioplasty of the right renal artery, the artery ruptured. Right in front of my eyes I witnessed it rupture. The radiologist expanded the balloon to slow down the bleeding, and they called the vascular surgeon on call who had just joined the hospital after finishing his fellowship. I talked to one of my partners, and we called an experienced vascular surgeon who was in another hospital a few minutes away. He had just finished a case, and he and his colleague came to Hillcrest Hospital where Donna was. An anesthesiologist friend came and evaluated the situation, looked at me, and shook his head. The vascular surgeon's colleague arrived first, evaluated Donna, and told me that she probably would not survive. I could not believe what was happening.

Donna: Weeks before I had the angioplasty, the Lord spoke to my heart and said that if I had the procedure something would happen. He didn't say what, but I had a knowing that something would go wrong. We met with the radiologist before we started, and he stated that it had been a long day and that he was tired. I was the last case of the day. I asked him, "If something goes wrong, will you be able to handle it?" He said that nothing was going to go wrong.

I laid on the X-ray table and above my head and to my side was a monitor. I watched as the catheter was threaded through my groin and into the artery of my left kidney. All went well. When it came to the right artery, I was watching again, suddenly I saw what looked like black ink being spilled and covering the screen of the monitor. It was the blood spilling out of the ruptured renal artery. I then asked if I was going to have to have surgery. Of course, the answer was yes. I remember being rushed down the halls on a gurney and going on an elevator. Then the last thing I remember was the abdominal pain. Throughout the whole ordeal, I never experienced fear and knew that this is what the Lord warned me about.

Don: I called our children and went to the doctor's lounge to wait for them. When I arrived in the lounge, an orthopedic surgeon friend, Dr. Al Holderness from the COF days and who was our Sunday school teacher at our church, came into the room. He shared that while doing evening rounds, he felt the Lord told him to go to the doctor's lounge. Just as I was being filled with fear, he arrived. He prayed with me, and I felt the peace of God. He stayed with me during the whole time of Donna's surgery. The presence of God was there, and I was able to be strong for Noel and Tammy when they arrived. The surgeon came in to see me after he was finished. He said it was as if a hand grenade had gone off in Donna's abdomen. She had lost a lot of blood, had to be transfused, and that they had to remove her right kidney. He related that it could be a stormy postoperative course but that she had survived. When my daughters and I were able to go into the recovery room, Donna was as white as the

FOLLOWING THE *Anointing*: PART II

bed sheets. Both daughters cried, and it was all I could do to hold it together. It was difficult seeing her so sick. I stayed overnight in the ICU, and by morning she had improved with a stable BP and the remaining kidney functioning well. She was moved to the general surgical ward, and I went home to get some rest. I now have a deeper understanding of the 23rd Psalm.

> **Psalm 23:4** Even though I walk through the valley of the shadow of death, I fear no evil, for You are with me; Your rod and Your staff, they comfort me.

Donna: I remember waking up in the ICU and couldn't believe what I saw. There was a tube in every place where one could be placed. There were IVs running in both arms and feet and one in my neck. There were machines running and bottles hanging everywhere. It was quite a sight.

Don: The postoperative course was challenging as multiple medications were necessary to control her blood pressure since they had only partially cleared the other kidney artery. Our daughter Jennifer, the nurse, took emergency leave from the Navy to come home and stayed with Donna in the hospital for the next week. At first, I was angry at my radiologist colleague who did the procedure. He had seen very few cases of this type, let alone treat it. I also felt helpless. Our Sunday class interceded for me, and their fellowship and prayers became so needed during that time. **The fellowship of believers is so important in our lives as we grow in Christ.** Donna was still very anemic and weak. The first few days she was so weak that it took five nursing staff to get her up with the multiple IVs and catheters. There was one funny incident that Donna will share.

Donna: It was my first time to get out of bed post-op, and I was very sedated. There were tubes and drains everywhere imaginable.

Kansas City and Return to *Tulsa*

One little aide was kneeling beside my bed to undo tubes fastened to it when my arm fell over the side of the bed and my hand cupped the top of her head. To this day I remember it like it was yesterday, and almost the only thing I remember about being in the hospital is what I said. I said, "Be healed in the name of Jesus." The whole room of people burst out laughing. I often wonder if there was anything wrong of which she needed to be healed.

Don: Many visitors came to the hospital and were amazed how pale and sickly Donna looked. She slowly improved and came home just in time for Thanksgiving and slowly regained her strength. Prior to her illness, I had a sense that I would be changing positions. One never knows where or how the enemy will attack to discourage you from following the Lord's leading, and he often uses situations in the family to accomplish his means. In the last few chapters and appendix of Part I[1] of our journey, we share how to look for weak points in your armor and how to do the spiritual warfare. An attack of this magnitude really made me look at my priorities.

I had a sense of wanting to return to YWAM in Hawaii, but there were no opportunities. Then an unexpected opportunity presented itself. In academic medicine in the Navy, the University of Chicago, and Loma Linda University, I had been involved in both basic and clinical research. Due to those connections, I was involved with some phase III clinical trials in IVF with a Swiss company, Serono. I enjoyed being involved with some investigational drugs in this rapidly developing field of reproductive medicine. As the treatment protocols improved in IVF along with tremendous advances in the laboratory, success rates were better than sixty percent in good centers. We were one of those centers. Because of that I had attended some Serono investigator meetings in Boston for multiple different treatment protocols that the company was presenting. It

FOLLOWING THE *Anointing*: PART II

was exciting to be involved in this cutting edge of clinical medicine. I was approached by the reproductive endocrinology vice president, Ernest Loumaye, from Geneva, Switzerland, who asked if I would be interested in coming to work as a medical director for Serono. They had multiple new drugs for which they needed medical directors to direct the clinical trials. I was surprised by this unexpected opportunity. Serono was a Swiss company, but this was a US position located in Boston, Massachusetts. Donna and I prayed about it, and I let them know that I would like to visit and interview. I took a few days off, and we flew to Boston. I had multiple interviews, and a realtor showed us around the area. We visited historic downtown Boston and the Navy shipyard at Charleston, Plymouth and really enjoyed our time there. Here I was praying about returning to YWAM and more ministry, but yet again an unexpected door seemed to be opening. It reminded me of the last time I was praying about returning to YWAM Kona, and the Lord opened up the door to Saudi Arabia. At age fifty-nine, I was considering slowing down from clinical medicine, especially after Donna's illness, but the thought of not doing surgery and no patient contact was hard to imagine.

Boston was too expensive for us, and I did not want to sell our ranch in Oklahoma. Two daughters were already living there, and the other two were wanting to return. Renting a place in Boston would be very expensive, and we found that it would be better to buy. I shared with the company that although I liked the job, I could not afford to live in the area since I was not planning to sell my Oklahoma residence. Also, Donna's parents were having medical issues in Arizona, and we anticipated that we would have to move them to Oklahoma for placement in an assisted living facility. Accepting the job would also mean that we would be separated for a good portion of the year.

CHAPTER 10

Working for Industry in *Boston*, *Switzerland*, and Return to YWAM

To my surprise I received an offer from the Biotech company for a decent salary, and they would provide housing for me in a condo on Boston bay for two years while I found a place to buy. Because of the difference in the cost of living with Oklahoma, they would provide a loan for a down payment of a house/condo that would be forgiven if I stayed employed with the company for five years. That was the formal employment offer I received one Friday afternoon. The next week Donna and I really pressed into the Lord in prayer asking for confirmation. I had been praying that if this opportunity was not of Him, that the door would close. There was also a concern about how it would all work with family demands. Was I following

FOLLOWING THE *Anointing*: PART II

His anointing where it seemed there would be no opportunities for ministry? Also, my salary was less than my current income, so the first year would be a struggle. Eventually, with bonuses in my contract based upon performance, the future looked better financially than staying in practice. It was also customary in the drug industry for all employees to sign an "at-risk contract" which meant I could be fired anytime without cause. God, was this really you leading, or was I being presumptive? Donna and I discussed this, but one thing we felt very strongly about our lives together is that we never wanted to look back and to say, "Oh if we had only done that." We continued to pray that if this opportunity was not of Him, that the door would close. The door stayed wide open. Did we have the faith to walk through it where it looked as if I was going farther away from my concept of how God had used me in the past? I never will forget, on the last day to return the contract, I dropped the signed contract into the FedEx drop box. Another step in my walk of following His anointing. I accepted the job as medical director and would be with the company for the next nine and a half years from January 2000 until July 2009. I would be leaving clinical medicine which I enjoyed.

I drove to Boston and found the condo in Marina Bay, Quincy, Massachusetts with instructions that included turning right or left at three different Dunkin' Donut stores. I had never heard of Dunkin' Donuts but was soon to become accustomed to this mainstay of New England life. Since the condo was near the bay in Quincy, it would become an ideal site to explore Boston. Donna came and helped me get settled. We fell in love with Boston, the patriotic history of the area, and its sports, especially the rivalry between the Boston Red Sox and the New York Yankees in the arena of baseball.

Working for Industry in *Boston*, *Switzerland*, and Return to YWAM

Shortly after I went to Boston, the Red Sox baseball team was sold, and the new ownership offered raffle entries in the local newspaper for the privilege to purchase a ten home game series. I entered, and surprisingly enough, I won and was able to purchase the ten game tickets along with a colleague from work. The first game I attended was against the New York Yankees. It was an exciting game, and I was hooked on major league baseball. Subsequently, all of my daughters would go to games and also become Boston fans. As of this writing, I still hold these tickets for another 20 years. My family would visit me in Boston, and Donna would come for a couple of weeks every three months or so, and I would go home for four to five days every other month. That became our lifestyle. Donna had to move her parents from Phoenix to an assisted living facility in Broken Arrow which added to her responsibilities of the demands of the one hundred-plus acre ranch. She also assumed the financial management of the ranch.

We found a new condo complex being built in Abington, MA which was twenty minutes from work. The company allow me to stay in the Marina Bay condo in Quincy for two years while the one in Abington was being built. The job was challenging and very demanding. I thought I was computer literate, but I had to develop better skills with spread sheets, pcs, and word-processing programs. I assumed the medical responsibility for clinical trials and because of my physiology degree, also was active with the discovery, basic science, and laboratory unit of the company. In this role I was also involved in business development evaluating new compounds. This resulted in me traveling to Cambridge and Manchester, UK. It was intellectually very challenging but also fulfilling. I struggled with why the Lord would lead me to industry, but I knew I was where I was supposed to be.

FOLLOWING THE *Anointing*: PART II

Crossroads Worship Center

The New England area has a rich Christian heritage which today is difficult to see. One of the first weekends I looked up church listings in the paper and yellow pages of the telephone book and ended up attending Glad Tidings Church in Quincy, the same town as the company condo. It was an Assembly of God church, and I felt at home. The minister was Rev. Greg Wheaten from New York. The church congregation was multicultural with long-term New Englanders and many Kenyans and Jamaicans who had come to Boston for education. I attended an adult Sunday school class taught by the associate pastor Karen Rydwansky's husband, Frank. Frank was a consultant for databases/management and also headmaster of a local Christian school. Frank and Karen became very close friends, and I believe the major reason I was in Boston was for this church. **The Lord shared with me that part of my purpose in being in New England was to pray, intercede, and reclaim His territory.** He also showed me how I have been used as a pioneer going into dry areas to demonstrate his power and presence. The church became the center of my life in Boston, and I felt very fulfilled there. The fellowship was fantastic, and Donna became a part of it when she would visit.

Frank and Karen eventually felt the Lord was calling them to establish a new church in the Weymouth area. Donna and I were in an initial group of twelve who felt the Lord was leading us to go with them to help establish the Crossroads Worship Center in Weymouth, MA. We were again helping to start another church. It was exciting. We began having services in Frank's school building and eventually were able to rent a property of our own in order to have a free-standing church. The Sunday morning, Sunday evening, and Wednesday evening services became the mainstay of

Working for Industry in *Boston, Switzerland*, and Return to YWAM

my existence in Boston. I became part of a small group and even started monthly healing services where we taught on healing. I was moving in ministry again. God was so good. Eventually in the 2020s the church would have a congregation of 700 for Sunday morning services in their own building. The following inserts from Pastor Karen Rydwansky and Reverend Anne Bates, associate pastor at the time, give insight to what the Holy Spirit was doing in people's lives as Donna and I followed His anointing.

Pastor Karen Rydwansky: As a church planter, I cannot stress enough the importance of having key people come alongside to help establish a new church. Don and Donna Tredway were in that category of key people who helped lay a solid foundation for lasting ministry. Their prophetic ministry and love for people enabled us to have monthly prayer services where focus on the work of the Holy Spirit brought about encounters with the Holy Spirit that changed lives and produced tangible results. Dr. Tredway's teachings were rich in the Word and practical for daily living. Don and Donna minister as a team and allow the gifts of the Holy Spirit to work through them in a beautiful complementary partnership. We are still reaping the blessing of their ministry and know God has rich ministry for them.

Rev Anne Bates: I remember the season that Don and Donna Tredway would come and minister at Crossroads Worship Center. We would hold special healing services on Sunday nights. The atmosphere was thick with anticipation of what God would do. Dr. Tredway would share scriptures and testimonies of how he witnessed the power of the Holy Spirit in his life and in the lives of others that would come across his path. He spent time increasing the faith in the room which would allow the Spirit of God to move freely.

FOLLOWING THE *Anointing*: PART II

Dr. Tredway was not a shouter but softly told of the goodness of God and how we could believe for great and mighty things from God. Every once and a while his voice would get loud, and the Holy Spirit would give him authority to speak a word over an individual. Often the person would shake or feel heat passing through them, and many would go out under the power of the Spirit. He would quietly move on and allow God to continue to minister through him. I can still see Dr. Tredway's face as he would look through the crowd. He was looking, and, I am guessing, asking God to guide him to the next person God wanted to heal or to impart a word of wisdom or knowledge. Dr. Tredway never wanted the credit for what was happening – he knew it was not out of his strength – but it was God's Spirit, and he always directed us to give God the praise. We cannot heal, only God can.

Donna was the same. She would often stay near Dr. Tredway as he ministered, until the Holy Spirit would speak to her and guide her to the right person. Donna's anointing, in my observation, was slightly different than her husband's anointing. Though God used her in the gifts of the Spirit, she also had a nurturing, motherly anointing that ministered to men and women alike. I remember one young adult who was covered with tattoos from head to toe sitting on her lap crying deeply as she held him and prayed in the Spirit. God was touching him and healing his heart.

Those healing services hold a special place in my heart. During that time, Dr. Tredway would often give me guidance as a new credentialed minister and encouraged me to pray for people. I know God used him to build my faith and believe for miracles. The Tredways have impacted my life through their ministry and also just by walking with them.

Working for Industry in *Boston, Switzerland*, and Return to YWAM

Don: Since the biotech company for which I worked, Serono, was a Swiss company, I began traveling to the corporate offices in Geneva, Switzerland. Donna even accompanied me a few times as I became more secure in the position. During one of my trips, I discovered that Bruce and Barbara Thompson were in charge of the YWAM base at Chatel, just outside Geneva in Rolla on Lake Geneva. It was just a short drive from Geneva. Donna and I visited Bruce and Barbara, renewing our ties with YWAM.

We still had our house in Kona which we had rented to close friends from our Crossroads DTS, Gary and Joann, for a dollar per month. He taught construction at the Kona base and also used his skills to make improvements on our house. They were considering buying a house, but we suggested that he build his house on top of ours. He did just that. He added a second story at his expense, and we ended up being co-owners of the property. We always had a place to stay when returning to Kona.

In time, Gary and his wife needed to return to their home in Southern California. We decided to sell the Kona house, and we considered buying a condo that was being built by YWAM right above the base. Three buildings were being completed with more to come, and we signed a contract on one that was to be completed in six months. Our house in Kona was an investment property, so we did what is called a 1031 exchange when it sold. That essentially meant that we had to invest the money from the sale of the house into another property at greater value within six months. To have a condo just above the base that we could rent out or just keep for the family seemed to be the appropriate move since I was being financially blessed in my job. Unfortunately, there were many delays, and we had to change building units on two different occasions (at a higher cost each time) in order to close within the six-month time

FOLLOWING THE *Anointing*: PART II

limit. We settled on a unit a few months later and flew to Kona to close. We met with the developer from YWAM and were informed that we could not close due to permit problems and that they could not give our down payment deposit until they resold the unit. I was very perplexed. Why did they allow me to fly all the way to Kona and take time off from work if they were aware we could not close on the condo? The president of the corporation found us a place to stay near the base and was very apologetic. I could not understand how this could happen. I was very upset with YWAM and told Donna that I would never return to Kona or YWAM again. Once again, I had been offended by the organization through which I had been released in God and came to know Him in a new way. **In my disappointment at the time, I thought only of the offenses, not the blessings.** My retirement plan of spending part of the year in Kona and the rest of the year in Oklahoma disappeared.

Fortunately, we had looked at another property in Oklahoma as a backup for the 1031 Exchange. It was a condo on Grand Lake one and a half hours from our home. It was a beautiful, two-story, three-bedroom, three-and-a-half-bath condo with a boat slip, garage, and apartment above the garage. The economic climate in the area was not good, and the price was very reasonable. We had only a month to close, so we flew back to Oklahoma and closed on the lake house. I was relieved that we were able to close in time but also disappointed about Hawaii. This condo was closer to home and, in reality, the better investment, as the family would also be able to enjoy it.

In early August 2004 I was on vacation at home in Oklahoma for a couple of weeks and planned to stop by Chicago on my return to Boston in order to visit an investigator of a compound for endometriosis that we were evaluating. I received a call from my stepfather

Working for Industry in *Boston*, *Switzerland*, and Return to YWAM

in southern Illinois that my mother was ill and hospitalized. Part I of my story that I have not shared was that several years after my father's death,[1] my mother began dating and eventually married my father's cousin, Bill Tredway. He was the youngest son of my grandfather's brother and had remained on the Tredway family farm (one hundred years in the family) to work the land and take care of his elderly parents. He had never married and had remained single. There was a fourteen-year difference in age between the two of them, my mom being older. They were concerned how I would react to their relationship and marriage, but I was very positive. Bill became the only grandfather that our girls ever knew, and the farm became an important part of their life growing up. My mother loved the farm and had many good years with Bill in her second marriage.

Mom's illness had progressed rapidly. She had become jaundiced (yellow skin) and was being evaluated by a gastroenterologist. I cancelled my trip to Chicago and rescheduled to fly to Southern Illinois. I arrived after the radiologist had done a biopsy of a mass around the gall bladder that came back positive for cancer. It had advanced so far that the surgeon felt it was inoperable, and the oncologist offered little hope in regard to chemotherapy. My mother was offered the opportunity to transfer to the University of Indiana hospital in Indianapolis for further evaluation, but she and my stepdad decided not to seek further treatment. For the next two weeks, Bill and I sat by the side of my mother's bed. It was very difficult for him as he adored my mother. I prayed and shared with her, but she was ready to go home to the Lord. She deteriorated quickly and died of renal failure at the age of eighty-four. As I sat by her bedside, the Lord spoke to me concerning a mother's love and revealed much of that part of His character to me. **The mother heart of God** is discussed in depth in the appendix chapter on the

FOLLOWING THE *Anointing*: PART II

Character of God in part one of our story.[1] This teaching would expand the depth of Donna and my ministry regarding the Holy Spirit in the years to come.

It was a difficult time for me after my mom's death as both of my parents were gone. I cherish the years that we were together and rejoice that they are with the Lord. After the funeral, Donna and the girls went back to Oklahoma, and I returned to work in Boston.

After my mother's death, Donna related to me something that my mother told her and that I did not know. It was that when she was pregnant with me in her last trimester, she had appendicitis. She was afraid that she would lose the pregnancy during surgery and had prayed, "Lord save this pregnancy, and I will give you the child." The Lord's hand had been on me all these years without me knowing it, for I was His and He had a plan for my life.

Romans 11:29 for the gifts and the calling of God are irrevocable.

During the years at Serono, I had a change in supervisors of our division of Reproductive Endocrinology and Infertility three different times. On two occasions I was asked to be the interim head of the division. The third time I asked to be considered for the position and became Vice President of the Clinical Development Unit of Reproductive and Metabolic Endocrinology. God had given me favor, and I prospered financially. The years we had sacrificed on the mission field, He made up for.

Luke 2:52 And Jesus kept increasing in wisdom and stature, and in **favor with God and men** (bold emphasis is mine).

For the next few years in my new position, I would travel a lot, being at least a week in Europe every month. Serono was sold

Working for Industry in *Boston*, *Switzerland*, and Return to YWAM

to Merck Germany, and there was quite a bit of unrest at work. I was now near the time of retirement, and I told the new owners that I would remain to help them through the transition if they wanted me to. All managers were interviewed, and I was reappointment to my VP position. Along with that came more responsibilities with employees in Darmstadt, Geneva, and Boston. It was a busy, challenging time as new structures were put in place, and I witnessed the company changing. It was quite a change to move from a company of five thousand to a worldwide company of over thirty thousand. I remember attending an executive meeting of 300 VPs from across the globe in Darmstadt, Germany.

While being blessed financially and enjoying management and scientific challenges, I questioned the Lord as to why I was working in the biotechnology industry. Yes, I enjoyed the development of the local church in Weymouth, being an elder and teacher, but I missed the public ministry. On one my trips to Geneva, at the airport I had to take a taxi to a management meeting in France. In the taxi, I noticed that the driver had Christian music on the radio. I used that as a means to open a conversation with him. I had a word for him that God was with him during his current struggles. He then shared with me that he was going through a difficult divorce, and as we arrived at my hotel, we prayed, and the presence of the Lord filled the taxi. God ministered to him while I was questioning God why I was there. **I wonder how many opportunities we miss when God has us right where He wants us.** Oh Lord, help us to be sensitive to your Holy Spirit and let us not miss opportunities in You.

On another trip to Switzerland, I found that Rev David De Carvalho from Hawaii had returned to YWAM and was now in Chatel Switzerland leading the base's YWAM schools of counseling as he had for a number of years in Makapala, Hawaii. Once again, I began

FOLLOWING THE *Anointing*: PART II

teaching a couple times a year at the Chatel base. I was in Geneva so often for my job that I could come a week early or late in order to teach at YWAM. Here I had thought that God had deserted me, but I watched Him minister again and again as I would share His word. Signs and wonders were still present because He was present. **The Lord had a plan for me, if I would only follow His anointing.**

My job was becoming more difficult. With the new company there was a change in how projects were approved and budgeted for our division. There was a three-man committee made of marketing, clinical (that was me), and manufacturing. Jean Pierre represented the manufacturing side. I had come to know him over the years and had enjoyed working with him. For the next few years my interaction with Jean Pierre became very difficult. If there was agreement in a meeting and Jean Pierre disagreed, he would continually come back to revisit the issue. For some reason that really irritated me, and he and I had many tenacious encounters to the point that others noticed it. My responses were in anger. I went to the Lord asking why I was responding that way. It took me a couple of years to work through it, but the Holy Spirit helped me to love and change my response to him. I now consider him a dear friend. **Has God brought a Jean Pierre into your life to teach you and to help you grow in His Character?**

Donna would periodically join me on trips to Switzerland, especially if I was going to teach in Chatel. I witnessed how the Lord opened doors for me to minister back into YWAM and also to individuals at my work as they were curious about my mission work. If I asked the Holy Spirit for opportunities to share, doors would open. I was using my tent making, just a Paul did, to be a witness to the reality of Jesus Christ – **Marketplace Ministry**. God was letting me see a different way to witness about Him.

Working for Industry in *Boston*, *Switzerland*, and Return to YWAM

I began seeing our research funds being diverted to other divisions instead of our division while our division sales were significant. Most was going to other divisions such as oncology. To work in the drug development in obstetrics, gynecology, and infertility requires multiple trials with large safety margins, especially obstetrics. Although we had some good compounds for obstetrical and gynecological problems, I noticed that the reinvestment into our division was not occurring. The handwriting was on the wall that my time was coming to an end. I had planned on one more year, but I received an offer to join my former supervisor in a new company based in Houston, Texas. They offered me good stock options and a decent salary, and I could work from home most of the time, only having to come to Houston a week a month. I really struggled if this was the Lord because I was tired of traveling. For the past year every month I spent three weeks in Europe, and I was exhausted. More changes were occurring in the company, and I was totally involved in never ending committee meetings and not into the research that I enjoyed. The company in Houston had two compounds that were in the areas of my interest. As I prayed, I could not get an answer. However the door was open, so I said to the Lord again, I am going through this door, and if it is not of you, close the door. I formally retired July 2009 from EMD Serono (subsidiary of Merk Germany) after nine and a half years at the age of sixty-eight. I had the usual retirement parties and felt remorseful for leaving the company, but I did not have the excitement for the job as before. I especially did not want to leave the church and the fellowship of the believers in the Boston area.

CHAPTER 11

Retirement from Medicine

The condo sold in Boston, and Donna came to help me pack to move the belongings back to Tulsa. I did not realize the fast pace at which I had been going. I was so exhausted but couldn't rest. I was used to being active, but now there was no more blackberry, no more being called at all hours, no multiple emails, and phone calls to Geneva and Darmstadt. Donna and I had to adjust because she was used to making decisions on her own as we had essentially been living apart for over nine years. The family was not used to having me at home either. Donna had her everyday routine as I did, and we were not part of the other's daily life. We had to adjust again to one another and learn to live together again not just for a week's visit. I had a hard time winding down. As soon as I got home, I received a call from the company in Houston. The major drug that they had was in final clinical trials and began having liver toxicity problems resulting in the FDA stopping the trial. I had been scheduled to attend a major investigator meeting for the company, but it was cancelled. Also, my job offer was withdrawn. I couldn't

FOLLOWING THE *Anointing*: PART II

believe it. All that I had planned was not coming to pass. Did I retire too soon? In addition, I had a hard time walking because of severe pain in my left knee. I was depressed – what was I going to do? God, did I miss you? Was I so anxious to go home that I moved ahead of God? Even to this day I believe I left Boston and Crossroads Worship Center before I should have.

I formed a consulting company in order to finish some reports and scientific articles about studies that we had done at EMD Serono. They hired me as a consultant, and I also did consult work for other companies. I was able to do all of this from home. My old company even had me go to Copenhagen for an experts' meeting on a new neurological drug. I was enjoying my consulting work and was actually very busy, usually without having to travel. This would continue for the next number of years. My left knee was giving me tremendous pain, and I had an arthroscopy to remove a torn meniscus. This was the beginning of medical treatments in addition to my long-standing high blood pressure.

When I retired from EMD Serono and the job with the Houston company fell through, I had wanted to return to teaching in Tulsa. I inquired about teaching at my old Department of Obstetrics and Gynecology at the University of Oklahoma, Tulsa Medical College. The school had expanded into a four-year medical school in conjunction with Tulsa University instead of a two-year clinical clerkship. I talked to the Dean, who was a former colleague, and even applied for the position of associate dean for the developing school. Nothing materialized from that, and to teach in my old department they wanted me to take clinical call as staff in the evening. Also, I could sense some reservations from the new department chairman when I offered my services. I even talked to the head of Physiology about returning to basic science and teaching as an adjunct professor, but they were fully staffed.

Teaching at a Junior College

I was then invited to the OSU School of Osteopathy in Tulsa to lecture to their residents. I thought this would be the avenue, but they would not give me an adjunct academic appointment with my strong academic background, even though I had one at the University of Oklahoma.

I then noticed that Rogers State University in Claremore was advertising for an adjunct professor to teach pharmacology for nursing students. I was offered the job and considered it, but I was having trouble with my right shoulder with two tears in the rotator cuff. I had this repaired and could not accept the position at Rogers State. During my shoulder recovery I noticed that Tulsa Community College (TCC) with four campuses (one of the largest community colleges in the US) was recruiting for the position of Department Chairman of Science and Math for the Southeast Campus which was near our home. It was a very good interview, and one member of the committee was one of my former patients. They asked me if I would plan to teach, and I shared with them that I would and also shared my love for teaching physiology. They had reservations since I had not been associated with TCC, and I did not get the position. I was not surprised, but then the provost and new chairman contacted me and asked me to apply to teach Physiology as an adjunct professor. I accepted and taught a second-year class on Human Physiology. I would be an adjunct professor at TCC starting the January 2011 semester through 2013. The classes consisted of nursing, pre-med, and biology students. I really enjoyed teaching, but initially I taught the same as if I was teaching medical students, and the first exam I

FOLLOWING THE *Anointing*: PART II

gave, the average score was thirty-five, so I had to adjust. I enjoyed the lectures and would give clinical correlations and always had ten essay questions on my exams, encouraging the students to apply their knowledge. I found many of the students did not like this type of exam, and I was surprised how many just wanted a grade without having to work for it. I gave extra credit for additional work and some thrived, but many did not. I really enjoyed this role and felt quite comfortable that this is where the Lord wanted me. I also began teaching an introductory first-year course of Human Anatomy and Physiology. The course was a lot of work and rapidly weeded out those floundering.

After my retirement in 2009 from the biotech industry, I felt the Lord say to me that my time was now His. Although I was teaching as an adjunct faculty at TCC, I continued to ask myself if this was the time that I would finally return to full-time ministry. I received a notice about YWAM Kona having a 50th year anniversary celebration in Kona at the end of November 2010. A few days before the celebration, Donna and Peter Jordan, our Crossroads DTS leaders, were having a meeting of YWAM Associates, an organization that they had established for YWAM alumni. Even though I had misgivings about returning to Kona after the condo situation, we wanted to see the Jordans and old friends. We stayed at the local hotel where the Associates Meeting was and enjoyed the time visiting, especially with Donna and Peter as they had such an impact on our lives.

They shared that they were leading an All Nations All Generations DTS starting in January in Kona. Donna had always wanted to be on staff of a DTS while I preferred to be just a teacher. The Jordans invited Donna to staff with them for the lecture portion of the DTS. She asked me, and all of a sudden, I said yes. That meant she would be gone for three months during the winter. I couldn't believe that

Retirement from Medicine

I said yes before thinking it through. I believe the Holy Spirit had prompted me to give the OK before I could think about the situation.

On the last day of the Associates Conference, we received a call from our daughter Kimberly in the Los Angeles area. Her husband Jon was an FBI agent and had recently returned from Afghanistan. He had started having severe headaches and had been admitted to UCLA Medical Center in the ICU. He had a dissecting aneurysm of the internal carotid artery. An MRI showed that the dissecting aneurysm was so high that the UCLA surgeons determined it was inoperable. The prognosis was not good. Kimberly was asking Donna to come and help take care of their two young children, Alex and Megan, while she traveled to and from the hospital. The Associates group prayed for him as did multiple prayer groups. His symptoms stopped, and an MRI six weeks later indicated no sign of the dissecting aneurysm. What an answer to prayer. Praise the Lord for His faithfulness.

While Donna was with Kim, I attended the 50th Kona Anniversary and enjoyed seeing all of the YWAMers from Switzerland, Australia, Asia, the US, and all the places that we had ministered. David and Kim De Carvalho were there from Switzerland. They had been invited to return to Kona for the January quarter to restart the Counseling School at the base. That same week he was also approached by the elders of Mokuaikaua Church, the first Christian Church in Hawaii, as to whether he would be interested in being considered for the position of interim pastor. The previous pastor had fallen from grace and was no longer there. The church needed healing, and the elders asked if he would be interested since he had been a congregational pastor on the Island before going to Switzerland. This would unfold during the next few months as he was committed to lead the counseling school for the January quarter 2011. He invited me to teach at the school in February on my favorite subject, the Holy Spirit.

After the 50th Anniversary Celebration, I returned back to Oklahoma, and Donna returned from Kimberly and John's house the middle of December. She still wanted to join the Jordans for the All Nations All Generations DTS and flew back to Kona to join the staff after the new year.

That winter was one of worse winters in the Tulsa area. I recall having snow drifts six feet high in my driveway. I had to get my tractor with a front loader to clear the driveway and the rural road to our house. All this time Donna was enjoying Hawaii while the animals and I suffered through frigid weather.

As previously noted, I was invited to teach for a week at the Foundations of Counseling School in Kona, led by David De Carvalho, during that January quarter. It was a precious time where the Lord would give me individual words for various students, and He demonstrated His presence again with signs and wonders. I also had a sense that the Lord was wanting us to return to Kona and to fulfill my desire of living part of the year in Kona and the rest in Oklahoma. A realtor showed us various condos, but nothing we saw witnessed to us to buy, and I had no desire to look at anything in Hualalai Village, the condos above the base, because of the bad experience we had there. I was in Kona for two weeks spending time with Donna and visiting her school. I knew very few people on the base at that time, and I was always introduced as Donna's husband, not as a YWAM teacher or former staff – quite a switch for me.

Donna: My identity has always been, "Oh, you are the doctor's wife," and it seemed that I had no identity of my own. I was on staff for the All Nations All Generations DTS for three plus months while Don was home in Oklahoma. YWAM holds Thursday evening services that are attended by all staff and students and are open for the public to attend. My dorm room was right above where the meetings were held, so at times my roommates and I would sit on the bed by the overlooking window to "attend the meeting." One Thursday evening as I was in our room listening to the service, I heard God tell me to go down to it. I didn't respond to the prompting at first until He repeated it two more times. At that, I thought that I had better go. At the meeting the speaker had the younger people pray for the older ones there. Someone came and prayed for me and then left to return to their seat. Then the speaker told the older ones to pray for the younger ones. God showed me a young lady in a far corner and told me to go to her and tell her that she was beautiful. I did, and when I gave her the message and prayed for her, she was slain in the Spirit. Then God showed me another person on the other side of the court and told me to pray for that person. I did, and that person, too, went down. This happened a third time, and by then people were lining up to be prayed for. God was having fun as there were people laying all over the floor. Such occurrences were not common in YWAM at that time, and by the end of the evening I was recognized, not seeking it, by many who were there. When Don came to visit me, the table was overturned as he was known as, "Oh, you are Donna's husband." That gave me great joy and a sense of my own identity.

Don: There was a two-week writers' seminar after Donna's school was finished that she decided to attend before returning to Tulsa. In this course she met Duane and Leeann Rawlins who were on staff of the seminar. Duane, a former realtor from Oregon, had purchased two condos in Hualalai Village that he was wanting to sell. Donna shared with him that we were looking for a condo, and he showed her their two. She fell in love with a three-bedroom, fully furnished, second-story end unit in a two-story building. She called me, sent me pictures, and wanted to buy it. She even had me talk to Duane who, of course, was very convincing. I could not believe it. There was no way we could afford this condo, and Duane had just rented it to David De Carvalho, who had stayed on in Kona having accepted the position of interim pastor at Mokuaikaua Church (May 2011). With the rent income we could afford to purchase the unit. The Lord told me to buy it from Duane and to help David and Kim De Carvalho by allowing them to live in it. We bought in the same complex where I said that I would never buy. **Never say never to God.**

For the down payment, I had to sell my Toyota Tundra pickup truck in Tulsa and then had difficulty obtaining a loan because the majority of the units owned by YWAM in the complex had never been finished. Eventually the broker found a lender, but the appraisal was less than Duane's selling price. Duane was not going to send his car back to the mainland from Kona and needed a car. With the Word of the Lord, I countered that if he would accept the appraised value of the house, I would give him our Camry Hybrid that was in excellent condition, in order to make up the difference. The value of the Camry was actually a few thousand dollars over the difference in loan value, but the Lord told us to honor Duane. He accepted the offer, closed on the condo, and we drove the car to him in Oregon. We became friends, as well as with Rev De Carvalho's landlord.

CHAPTER 12

YWAM Kona, Medical Discipleship Training School (MEDTS) 2012

As the Lord had laid on Donna and my heart to buy this condo, He also told me not to schedule myself to teach in the January 2012 semester at TCC. I could not understand why, but the message was very clear. During the fall semester of 2011, Dr. Bruce Thompson called and shared that a group of Korean physicians had approached Loren Cunningham about starting a Medical DTS for healthcare professionals, especially physicians. They had related to Loren that Korean physicians had to retire at age sixty-five and many Christian physicians wanted to go to the mission field. Loren called Bruce Thompson and asked if he and Barbara would lead a Medical DTS starting in January 2012. Bruce then asked Donna and me to assist them. It was short notice, but now I understood why the Lord told me to keep the January semester clear. We prayed and felt that we were to go and planned to return to Kona.

The University of the Nations had a worldwide leadership meeting in Kona during the fall of 2011. I took time off from teaching and returned to the island to attend the meeting and to look for housing as our condo was rented. Barbara and Bruce were also looking and the four of us decided to rent and share a large three-bedroom condo in Hualalai Village. I also bought a used car from another YWAMer which we let the De Carvalho's use when we were not in town. Everything was falling in place. With only a few months to prepare, the Thompsons and we planned for the upcoming school, and Bruce assembled an amazing staff.

During the time of preparation for the Medical DTS (MEDTS), I was contacted by the biotech company from Houston, Repros (the same company that had offered me a position when I retired from EMD Serono), and was again offered the position of Chief Medical Officer. My former boss from Serono was no longer working there, but the same CEO was. Serono had evaluated their product but had decided not to license their compound. Repros had restructured after bankruptcy and had finished a phase II study under the direction of the FDA. They had received a green light from the FDA to proceed. I was impressed by what they had done, and they agreed to pay for some of the promises made before. I could also do a majority of my job remotely, only being in Houston a few days a month. It seemed like a good group, and I liked the products they were developing because they were of the same class that we had evaluated at Serono. I also believed this was the Lord providing finances for our mission work, so I accepted the job and began my work remotely from Hawaii.

YWAM Kona, Medical Discipleship Training School (MEDTS) 2012

In the first few weeks of the school, the enemy attacked at home with issues arising with our children, especially our youngest, and Donna wanted to leave the DTS and return home. The intercession of the Thompsons kept us there and allowed the Lord to work in our daughter's life. Family issues of one type or another at the beginning of a DTS would become a recurrent theme in our lives for the next several years. The enemy will always try to attack when we are following God's anointing. We must be alert and stand firm against his tactics.

> **Ephesians 6:11** Put on the full armor of God, so that you will be able to stand firm against the schemes of the devil.

Our first school was composed of twenty-one students. It was multinational, multicultural, and taught bilingually in English with Korean interpretation. Like all YWAM's DTSs, we followed the established content of subjects for the three-month lecture phase that covered topics such as Hearing God's Voice, Knowing God, the Holy Spirit, the Father Heart of God, Spiritual Warfare, and Intercession. A two-and-a-half-month outreach followed the lecture phase with three teams being sent out: one to Haiti, one to the Philippines, and the other that went to both China and North Korea. After, the outreach all teams returned to Kona for a week of debriefing. What an exciting time this first year was in pioneering the school. It was exciting to see the growth in the students in what they had been taught during the lecture phase. When the school was over, we returned home to Oklahoma, and I returned to teaching at TCC for the remainder of the year. It had been a very busy school, and I enjoyed teaching again in the DTS. I saw opportunities opening again in Hawaii.

FOLLOWING THE *Anointing*: PART II

Bruce had a very unique way of uniting the class and building trust from the first day of a DTS. He used what are known as The Quaker Questions. These questions allowed students and staff to share about themselves and to build up trust within the group. All would answer the first question before going to the next. The four questions were: (1) Where did you live between the ages of five and twelve? (2) How was your home heated? (3) Who was the center of warmth in your life? (4) When did God become real to you? I was amazed how God used these questions for each school. They were certainly icebreakers and were an excellent way to start the school. Year after year we saw the Holy Spirit move and minister during these questions. **Try them yourself and see if the Holy Spirit speaks to you.**

I flew from Hawaii to New York during the last month of the school's lecture phase in order to attend Repros investors' meeting. The CEO presented the data from the dose-finding study and was trying to convince the audience to invest in the development of the drug. I had done some presenting for Serono and EMD Serono and knew how critical this was for a small biotech company. The CEO was a very controlling person, and I soon had the sense that he needed my name with my qualifications and history of working for big pharma mainly for the investors. I will talk more about this later.

After a few days in New York, I returned to Hawaii for the last month of the school. During the outreach a staff member would do a pastoral visit to see how the students and staff were doing. Donna did the pastoral visit to Haiti. I returned to teaching at TCC and returned to Kona for the outreach debriefings. Bruce shares about the school.

YWAM Kona, Medical Discipleship Training School (MEDTS) 2012

Dr. Bruce Thompson[11]: Dr. Don and Donna Tredway played a vital part in pioneering and developing the Medical Discipleship Training School (MEDTS) in 2012 in Kona Hawaii at the University of the Nations campus. The vision for this school was initially sparked by a number of healthcare professionals who approached Loren Cunningham about launching a school to help colleagues into medical missions.

Don and Donna's background greatly helped to recruit students into the school. Don had been Chairman of the Ob/Gyn dept. at Oral Roberts University Medical School in Tulsa, Oklahoma, USA. He also spent a number of years in research on infertility with various drug companies. Donna was an RN before her family came along.

During the school we not only had deep teaching on knowing God and making Him known but also classes focused on mission medical practice and principals. Subjects such as tropical diseases, vaccinations, nutrition, and a wholistic approach for the field were covered.

The Tredways taught on the Holy Spirit and His gifts. Through their anointed ministry many students were baptized in the Holy Spirit, while others repented over sins and experienced deliverance. Don had an anointing that saw many slain in the Spirit while Donna had a gift in facilitating discernment and deliverance from strongholds the enemy had in students' lives.

Students' lives were turned upside down during the schools, and many went out after the three months together on a two-month outreach to various medical missions on land and on ships. The reports that came back with the students were amazing. A pediatrician saw a child raised from death as the team prayed for him. Other healings and deliverances occurred as they worked with all

FOLLOWING THE *Anointing*: PART II

the skills in which the Tredways had been training them. A dentist and his family went out to Iraq and stayed there. A doctor went to join in a hospital in Iraq and stayed for two years.

Eventually Don and Donna took over the school leadership, training others to carry it on. They have made an awesome investment for the Kingdom in lives from all over the globe. Over the years it has been an honor and privilege to work with them.

Don: We had an amazing staff in the first school that included a psychiatrist, Dr. Paul Rodriquez. He was a Cuban emigrant who had had accepted Jesus as his savior, gone to Bible school, and eventually to medical school. He was a seasoned physician with significant spiritual insight. Paul would become a close friend who would help me walk through some of my physical trials that were to come. Paul gives some insight about the first MEDTS.

Dr. Paul Rodriquez: In September 2011, I had the rare honor of meeting and getting to know Dr. Donald Tredway. Later that year, and for the first quarter of 2012, my spouse, Cathy, and I worked with Don and his spouse, Donna, in staffing the first Medical Discipleship Training School in Kona, HI.

When it comes to the work of Christ's Spirit in us, I have learned that, although He indwells every believer, His special anointing and empowerment in us requires a firm conviction on our part. This is a conviction that flows out of a persevering faith in our Lord's character, goodness, might, and infinite and unconditional love for us. And I am convinced that this conviction opens the door to our Lord's anointing.

During my work with Don Tredway, I witnessed the power of Christ's anointing in him – an anointing that came from Don's firm, personal conviction. Whether Don felt it or not, I witnessed the healing and moving impact this anointing has had on others. I have experienced the Lord's Spirit moving through Don – as a faithful channel for our Lord – imparting the faith, hope, and courage we all need to have real and sustainable victory in our lives.

The life of suffering that I know Don has lived reminds me of

Philippians 3:10 That I may know Him and the power of His resurrection and the fellowship of His sufferings...

To me, it reveals the reason Don has so known our Lord and has walked so closely with Him throughout the years and the reason he possesses the requisite conviction. I have been unspeakably grateful for Don's faithfulness and true friendship and for this experience that has so consistently and memorably glorified our Lord Jesus Christ.

Don: This is the principal of the courses at University of the Nations and YWAM. To have a time of application of what you have learned during the lecture phase is such an important principal. If His Word is true and Jesus is Lord of your life, it will result in your life being changed. It also seemed that Donna and I had reached our goal finally of living part of the year in Hawaii and the rest in Oklahoma.

After that first MEDTS, I was invited to teach in a DTS at the YWAM Mendocino Coast base in California. A member of the staff had been a student at the Counseling School in Chatel, Switzerland where I had shared a few years earlier. The base was starting a school of the Supernatural and wanted me to come and speak to a regular DTS about the Holy Spirit. Donna and I flew into San Francisco and then had a long trip up the coast to the Mendocino area. The class was small, and most of the time was spent with individual counseling and ministry. That is Donna's anointing, and I assisted her. It was a good time of rest for us, and we appreciated the base. It had been a hippy camp in the fifties that God reclaimed for His use.

Later in the year we taught at a bilingual English/Korean Counseling School in Hawaii under the leadership of Eunsook Kim. Again, God ministered to the students with words of knowledge and signs and wonders. Eunsook introduced us to Malsoon Park who later became our Korean interpreter and an important part of the MEDTS team in the years to come.

Eunsook Kim: Dr. Tredway relies on God to identify His heart for people to which he ministers. Don waits patiently for information that God downloads to him in order to bring the Father's Heart to people. He resists getting pre-notice information for people because that might hinder his perception to listen fully to God. Dr. Tredway and Donna are very cautious not to intercept their perception by other information but try hard to get God's Word to bring His healing, comfort, and encouragement. What I hear repeatedly from them is that they want to bring glory to God through their ministry.

Onnuri Church Seoul, Korea 2012 (Awesome Presence of God) and YWAM Perth, Australia

Don: Dr. Bruce Thompson had been invited to speak at the annual 2012 Recovery Conference (Sep. 19-21) at Onnuri Church in Seoul Korea. Bruce had spent many years teaching in Korea on the Plumbline[11] and had touched many lives. He was unable to attend the conference and recommended that they invite me. I received an invitation to be one of their three main speakers for the three-day conference. It was a surprise and honor for me. I corresponded

YWAM *Kona*, Medical Discipleship Training School (MEDTS) 2012

with them that I usually spoke on the Holy Spirit and not on the subject of the conference. They responded back that they would like me to speak on the Holy Spirit. Onnuri Church was one of the major churches in Korea with many branches in Korea and worldwide. I was a bit intimidated since it had been a while that I had spoken to large groups and had only recently begun ministering to YWAM schools.

I also received an invitation speak to a midwife school and DTS in Perth, Australia. In September Donna and I flew to Australia, stopping in Sydney to visit with Ern and Lyn Crocker and then on to Perth. It was good to see Sydney again and to catch up with our dear friends. We also had a wonderful time at the base in Perth. We taught in the two schools, and once again God ministered to His people. We finished our time in Perth with a community meeting at the YWAM base in which God had me share my revelation of Him through the death of my father. Multiple people came forward to experience the Father Heart of God – what a blessing.

We then had a long flight from Australia through Japan to Seoul, Korea. It was the first time for us to visit Korea. I had been off the coast of Korea during the Viet Nam War at the time of the Pueblo incident but had never been in the country. At the airport we were met by a former Korean YWAMer who was now on staff of the church. He had been one of the students at Makapala where God had moved in a mighty way. He related how the presence of God was so strong at Makapala in the front row that he would purposely sit in the back. The Lord had me call him up to the front, but as he stood, he was slain in the Spirit. That experience was early in his walk with God and changed his life. I was again amazed how God orchestrates and how this individual was one of my hosts at the church a number of years later in Korea. He took us to an apartment complex where we met another member of the church, Youngmi, who had a condo in the complex. She was a gracious host who housed us in a guest apartment and took very good care of us during our time in Seoul.

The day after our arrival we met the senior pastor, associate pastors, and some other members of his leadership. That evening we attended the general meeting in the main auditorium which held several thousand people. It was overwhelming after coming from teaching classes of thirty people. I had been asked to teach two elective afternoon sessions of around one hundred people and two general sessions. The next afternoon I began to speak on Inner Healing in a session meeting with pastors' wives. The room was packed with 150 people. Shortly after the meeting began, the presence of the Lord came into the room, and a young lady a few rows back from the front started crying very loudly. Donna walked over to her, and the Holy Spirit had Donna hold her on her lap. The lady began crying like a small child, and the Spirit of the Lord filled the room when multiple ladies began to cry. As Donna was ministering to the one lady, I witnessed the Holy Spirit ministering to others. Multitudes were slain in the Spirit, and I will never forget the face of the associate pastor who was translating for me. I literally watched as God ministered to His people, healing them and setting others free. His presence was like a thick cloud in that room and continued for several hours. The next afternoon we had another session with the pastors' wives and ministered on the Mother Heart of God (the Holy Spirit), and Spirit of God moved again.

Some of the Korean students from the MEDTS and the All Nations DTS where Donna had been on staff met with us one afternoon at Youngmi's apartment. It was good to see how respective and gracious the Koreans are and how appreciative they were of Donna's time as staff. God had used her to affect many lives during the DTS.

The second morning I was to speak in the general meeting, the same auditorium that held several thousand people. I was nervous because the Lord had told me to speak on deliverance. I was taken directly to the podium, and as I looked up, the two-level auditorium was filled. I was uncomfortable with the subject, and now, the size of the audience. Then something amazing happened. For a number of years, God would at times show me faces of people before I would minister. When I saw the face in a prayer line, it would give me an extra measure of faith to minister to the individual. That morning in Seoul, God showed me the four Asian faces that He had previously shown me several years before. As I looked at the front row, those four faces were sitting right in front of me. Faith from on high filled me. God had me speak out commands of deliverance, not to various individuals, but over the entire congregation – something I had never done before. God's presence filled the room, and multiple people were set free by the power of God.

The next evening, I spoke at the general session on the Power of God and what He taught me about His love for me through the death of my father. Many were healed of their misconceptions of the Father Heart of God. What an awesome God we have. It was during that trip that the Lord confirmed that He had given me a heart for Asia. I had been to Asia with the military during the Viet Nam War and witnessed the cruelty of mankind and the ineptitude of governments. This time I witnessed deliverance of God's people through the saving and healing grace of Jesus Christ.

> **Hebrews 2:14-15** Therefore, since the children share in flesh and blood, He Himself likewise also partook of the same, that through death He might render powerless him who had the power of death, that is, the devil, and might free those who through fear of death were subject to slavery all their lives.

FOLLOWING THE *Anointing*: PART II

John 10:9-10 I am the door; if anyone enters through Me, he will be saved and will go in and out and find pasture. The thief comes only to steal and kill and destroy; I came that they may have life and have it abundantly.

I returned to Tulsa and finished the year's semester teaching at TCC and began to have thoracic back pain. Spiritually this was very difficult for me since God had healed my back in 1977 and had brought me into a close fellowship with Him. I struggled for a while praying but then took my X-rays and MRIs to two neurosurgeons for review. One was a former colleague from ORU who had treated me conservatively for a prolapsed thoracic disc a few years earlier. The old lumbar fusion which God had healed was stable, but the lumbar fusion resulted in increased stress to higher areas such as the thoracic area. Recall, I had also had cervical disc issues at Loma Linda. He noted problems again in the cervical as well as in the thoracic area. I also had an evaluation by a very experienced neurosurgeon who reviewed my films and was more concerned about the cervical area. I wanted conservative treatment, so he referred me to a pain control doctor who began giving me steroid injections every three to four months in the sac around the spinal cord in the thoracic area. The injections gave me tremendous relief and allowed me to function and to even go on an outreach to Iraq.

As the Chief Medical Director for Repros, I would have to travel between Broken Arrow and Houston. I needed a place to stay while in Texas, so Donna and I found a condo and signed a contract. I familiarized myself with the job, interacted with the staff, evaluated the trial that was to begin, and gave medial input. The CEO was very involved in all issues, and I had a sense he was uncomfortable with me. We had a frank discussion about my missionary work with YWAM that required me to be in Hawaii the first three months of the year and also my part-time teaching at the community college (TCC). I asked whether I could continue both, and he assured me that I could, but I noted some reservations. I prayed about our interaction as I was trying to work out my priorities and decided that I would resign from the adjunct position at TCC so I could concentrate on the Repros position and the MEDTS. A few days later during a protocol discussion, the CEO was wanting to take some shortcuts to shorten the length of the clinical trial. I disagreed and wanted to be more conservative in the approach, which would result in the trial being longer but with less risk. He got very angry before the group and stormed out. Everyone else seem to take this reaction in stride and told me he reacted that way sometimes. I had not shared with him that I was going to stop my TCC teaching and had also bought a condo. I probably should have gone back to him, but thought I would wait until he cooled down. The next day he advised me that it was not going to work for me as Chief Medical Officer and fired me. I asked if we could discuss his decision, but he said no. He had arranged for me to see the Chief Financial Officer for my severance package which he had already worked out. I had just signed a contract for a condo in the Woodlands area of Houston. The owner and real estate agent for the condo was very understanding and released me from the contract. The whole episode was quite a disappointment, but I trusted that the Lord was still in charge. I still believe God opened the doors to that company for a specific reason but that it was not fulfilled. I have asked for forgiveness for missing it and have tried through email with the CEO. I am not sure how it was received. I am still disappointed and believe that I missed what the Lord had for me in Texas. I did not resign from my teaching position at TCC, and in December, Donna and I returned to Hawaii to assist the Thompsons in the 2013 MEDTS.

CHAPTER 13

Medical Discipleship Training School (MEDTS) Kona 2013

The 2013 MEDTS was an exciting one with twenty-five students. Eleven were Korean, so again the course was bilingual. I taught on the Ministry of Jesus[1] and had a handbook that was a summary of various teachings that the Lord had given me over the years. The Holy Spirit had taught me to study the ministry of Jesus. He showed me that any personal experience must be based on and evaluated by His Word. **This combination of life experiences and the Word released tremendous power of God.** The more I learned of God's character, the more I realized and understood God's love for Don Tredway, and the more secure I was in Him. His presence would be with me as never before. That is key to being used of God. It fulfills the proclamation of Loren Cunningham for YWAM, "To Know Him and to Make Him Known." It is so simple when we realize it, but I had to have a lot of inner healing from the experiences of life in order for this to happen. This fulfills the scripture.

> **2 Corinthians 5:17** Therefore if anyone is in Christ, he is a new creature; the old things passed away; behold, new things have come.

In 2012 another YWAMer told me about a Dr. Bob Doe and his ministry as a prison physician in Lancaster, Pennsylvania. I contacted him and invited him to attend our first MEDTS, but he was unable to until our second school in 2013. Bob is quite a visionary and is a tremendous networker of people and ministries. I was amazed at this gift of God. He also had been working with the Kurdish people in Iraq for ten years and wanted to send a team to Iraq for the outreach phase of the DTS. In my morning prayer time, the Lord spoke to me to go as the staff member to Iraq with Dr. Doe and a team.

Dr. Robert Doe: Another special memory was our outreach trip to Kurdistan of Iraq. Prior to coming to DTS, I had already been engaged in health training and outreaches to the Kurdish Regional Government. When enrolling in the MEDTS, I requested that we be allowed to do an outreach to that region. Although not initially officially approved, a small group of us led by Dr. Tredway were given the green light to make that our destination. I specifically remember the day that Dean Sherman prayed for the outreach teams. The Iraq team did not initially get called up. As I was leaving to go back to my room, suddenly the call to the Iraq team came. Dean began with a prophetic word that the Kurds have been mistreated and rejected for generations and now God would turn his face toward them. The word continued by declaring that our group would be like fathers to the nation that would one day be birthed. This unique moment set that table for an incredible trip that year and for official Med DTS for the next two years.

On the trip with Dr. Tredway, we had incredible opportunity to connect directly with the Department of Health leaders and be invited to engage in teaching and training. Dr. Tredway was asked to consult about the Obstetrics program and the region even to the point of visiting an OB/GYN hospital under construction. One further surprise developed. The wife of the Director General of Health was involved in IVF, which was a specialty area of Dr. Tredway, and he helped pioneer that field in the USA.

In the following year on another outreach, students were allowed to operate the medical system in a Syrian refugee camp, teach, train in various sectors of the hospitals in Duhok, and generally have opportunities to pray with both patients and leaders. The final year, our team was able to teach medical students at the University of Kurdistan Hewler. Overall, prior to political and economic unrest in the region, we had many open doors and favor to influence the Kurdish Health system from the perspective of the Kingdom of God.

Don: On our way to Iraq, we had a long layover during the day on 15 May 2013 in Zurich, Switzerland. Bob had ministry friends, Stiftung Schleife,[12] close to Zurich, so we took the train and spent the day with them. The founders of the ministry were Geri and Lilo Keller who were very instrumental in the early days of the charismatic revival in Switzerland. Their son, Andreas Keller, was now in charge of the ministry along with the cofounder of the counseling part of the ministry, Werner Tanner. As we all met together, the Lord gave me a word for Andreas. Bob Doe recorded this event.

Dr. Bob Doe: A Wednesday word by Andreas Keller was given to Don Tredway while visiting their ministry in route to the Kurdish area of Iraq. God had given Don a word to Andreas about their ministry of how there was an opportunity before them that they were not to

FOLLOWING THE *Anointing*: PART II

discount but prayerfully consider for it was not as it seemed at first glance. It would result in the establishment of a part of their ministry that had never been fulfilled since the foundation of the ministry.

After this word was given, Andreas said that he had a word for Don also and to wait a moment while he got something from his office. He returned with an old serial number metal label from a Studebaker car. He had taken it off an old car sixteen years earlier (when Don went to Saudi Arabia) in South Carolina while working for Morning Star Ministry. He said that label was like Don. It represented the power of God from the past but where the label was worn off and shiny, it represented the new supernatural power of God that He was going to release. He said that Don knew His old glory and was a part of it in the past, but Don was going to be one of the ones He used to release his power to a new generation. Andreas also related that the presence of God just oozed from Don's pores. He then asked Don to pray for them and for the release of this new power of God in their ministry.

Studebaker Label.

Dr.'s Fiddler, Doe, and Tredway (left to right) with Kurdish Administrator at Hospital in Iraq Outreach. 2013.

Don: That word was quite a surprise for me, but I could identify with it while not really understanding its significance. God had other surprises for me during that school. We were in a combined meeting with another school in a YWAM Associates meeting (Peter and Donna Jordan). The teacher was a prophetic physician from Canada, Dr. David Damian, who was also Director of Watchman for the Nations. He was being used of the Lord in Reconciliation and would have major meetings in Hong Kong, Australia, and other nations. With the creation of the MEDTS, the Lord spoke to Bruce Thompson and me to begin sharing again the vision for a whole person clinic on the base with an outreach to the community. We had both shared this vision again during this meeting with David Damian for which an offering was taken. I had just shared and sat down when the Lord spoke to me that, "You are to share the vision, but you will not fulfill it." I was shocked for I was accustomed to bringing things into being. Before I could contemplate this anymore, Bob Doe came up to me and said that God had told him to complete the vision of the clinic. He will tell us about the establishment of the Clinic in Hawaii.

Dr. Bob Doe: Haggai prophesied that it was time to build God's house, not to build our own houses. Cyrus had released the Jews to rebuild the Temple of God in Jerusalem. After finishing the foundation, opposition rose up for a number of years and the work was not able to be finished. Many became comfortable building their own houses while God's house remained in ruins. Haggai challenged the leaders to begin again and finish the work. I will share my story of Medical DTS and hopefully reveal the similarity between the Haggai story and healthcare for YWAM Kona.

I am a family/emergency/urgent care physician who had spent his entire career in Lancaster, Pennsylvania. In the early 1990s,

FOLLOWING THE *Anointing*: PART II

the Lord apprehended me while involved in a healthcare reform political journey and redirected me to ministry in a prison and numerous medical mission trips to the nations. During the travels and the work of ministry, I constantly encountered YWAMers who were always encouraging me to go to Kona for a DTS. In 2012, Drs. Tredway and Thompson started a Medical DTS. Many of my YWAM contacts "pressured" me to attend this school. Another leader from the school on counseling (Deborah Nakora) also invited me to Kona to "check it out." In 2012 I attended the Associates Week, which was working with the first Medical DTS, and met the leaders.

Returning back to Lancaster, I knew that it would likely be impossible for me to leave my job in urgent care for the local hospital and be gone for five months to the DTS. In addition, I was the chairman of Light of Hope CSO, a local ministry working with several innercity churches in Lancaster. We had just renovated a large church property to be used as an outreach center for counseling and healthcare in the city of Lancaster. All of this would clearly prevent me from going to Kona for DTS. However, the Lord arranged various circumstances that cleared the way for me to be a student in Kona in 2013. The assumption I had was that I would enjoy a sabbatical and then return to Lancaster to complete the counseling and healthcare project there. He did give a word about the project I was leading in Lancaster called the Connection Center. It was compared to Noah's Ark. I was to build it; He would fill it, and it would float when revival came.

At about the halfway point in the lecture phase of the DTS, we again had Associates Week, and David Damian was the speaker. Two unexpected events happened that week. First, we began to pray for various locations around the world where God would raise up counseling and healthcare models. A crazy thought came to me that

Medical Discipleship Training School (MEDTS) Kona 2013

these prayers were "not for me" since I was assigned the project in Lancaster. However, the Lord impressed the following thought in my heart. "Your vision was too small; I want you to play a role in catalyzing many places of healing and refuge (Arcs) around the world. Lancaster is just one and would have kept you tied down." Later in the week, Dr. Thompson and Tredway shared the YWAM healthcare vision that had started early on in Kona with Loren Cunningham's vision of "Twins" – training centers around the world and ships carrying healthcare to the nations. Later the twins were expanded to represent ships and land-based whole person healing models. Dr. Tredway specifically shared several disappointments over that prior couple of decades that prevented a whole person care clinic from rising up in Kona and the loss of Mercy Ships from YWAM control. He mentioned that YWAM Ships had recently resurrected the vision of ships; a campus health service had been started, but still the vision of whole person care systems serving the people of Hawaii was missing from fulfilling the vision. As he finished sharing, the Holy Spirt "tapped my heart" and said, "it is your job to finish this piece." Caught off guard by this word, I knew that I would have to respond to this invitation. I approached Dr. Tredway to share this thought, and his response was a matter of fact, "I knew that you would be the one."

It took two years to open the first step in achieving the vision of whole person care in Kona. We have now been open for five years and are employing more than six providers and twenty other staff. Dr. Tredway has served as the chairman of the board for this organization known as Transformation Health Network. As I write this memory, we are preparing for a new local Hawaii board of directors and a new position for a Practice Manager. All of these changes are being implemented to set a secure foundation that will allow expansion of the vision into mental health, addiction treatment, and integrative medicine. In addition, we have become a we-based training seminar in the areas of supernatural healing and deliverance as well as prophetic ministry that can be applied to patient care. Secondary health and healing schools and seminars area being planned.

I will always cherish the role of father that both Dr. Tredway and Dr. Thompson played in my life. Although not much younger than them in chronological sense, they have guided and supported me through many of the struggles that we have encountered along the way. I will always remember Dr. Tredway's word that he was only to start sharing the vision again and God would do the rest. Without the Medical DTS this would not have happened. In addition, many of our workers have come through the School. Please pray with us for the continued expansion of the whole person model and further completion of the vision and for Kurdistan to open again to our teams.

Don: There have been many challenges with starting the clinic. Dr. Park, a long time Korean pediatrician on the Big Island, was very instrumental in establishing the clinic. He worked long hours in addition to financially assisting along with others in the early days. Many had to help the first few years to make sure payroll was made for the clinic. The clinic would assume a lot of my time as I assisted Bob mainly as a sounding board as he learned how to manage a practice where Holy Spirit-directed whole person medicine was practiced. Many mornings for the next few years, Bob and I would have morning coffee together discussing the Medical DTS, the clinic, and other challenges. Bob would teach intercession in many of the schools as well as lead the teams to Iraq.

Medical Discipleship Training School (MEDTS) Kona 2013

This year Donna also did the pastoral visit to the team in the Amazon. She will tell us about that outreach.

Donna: There were two doctors and a dentist on the team. We held clinics in jungle villages and made do with rather primitive conditions in setting them up. There were times of playing with the children and visiting with the adults and sharing about the love of Jesus.

MEDTS, Students and Staff, 2013.

Ministry Father Heart of God MEDTS, 2014.

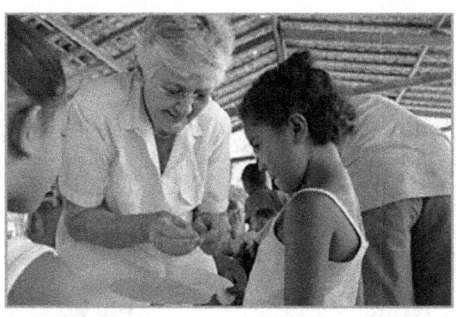

Donna Outreach in Amazon MEDTS, 2018.

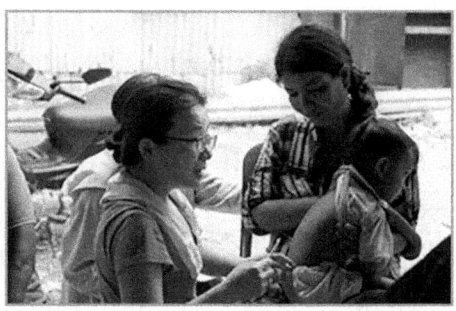

Outreach Cambodia MEDTS, 2013.

FOLLOWING THE *Anointing*: PART II

Don: I returned to Tulsa after the 2013 DTS and was asked to teach Human Physiology in the summer session. It was a small class of eight but one of the best classes that I've ever had. I found it a pleasure to teach them as they were intent to learn. The majority of the class received As, which was unusual for my class since I stress critical thinking and physiology is an applied science. That summer I was approached by the Associate Dean for Science and Math and was encouraged to apply for a full-time academic position and to be the lead faculty for the first-year course of Anatomy and Physiology. They would still allow me to continue teaching the second-year course of Human Physiology which was my passion. I had reservations because of the MEDTS in January 2014 and a teaching trip that I had scheduled in September to return to Seoul, Korea. I could take the time off for the Korea trip, but I could not be gone for three months starting in January. I went through the academic process of applying and prayed that the Lord would block it if it was not of Him. We were on vacation in Boston when I received a call from the dean that my application was approved, but as customary for TCC, I was only given an academic title of Assistant Professor of Biology. That was quite a letdown for me after being a tenured associate professor at the University of Chicago and a full professor at ORU, Loma Linda University, and the University of Oklahoma. I believe the dean thought I would turn it down (which I have to admit was my first response), but I called back and accepted the position. I felt God was again dealing with my pride. If He was calling me to go to TCC, did it make any difference in what my academic rank was? I became a full member of the department and had four wonderful years (2013-2016) teaching full time to the younger generation. I would only be a one-week guest lecturer for the MEDTS during those years.

Medical Discipleship Training School (MEDTS) *Kona* 2013

Onnuri Church Seoul, Korea 2013
(Manifest Love and Presence of God)

I had received an invitation from one of the associate pastors to return to Onnuri Church for the next annual recovery conference, the theme being "The Presence of the King." I would be one of the main speakers with Leanne Payne's group[13,14] for morning and evening sessions. I had arranged for a replacement lecturer for my classes at TCC, and Donna and I flew to Seoul. We arrived on Saturday, a few days ahead of the conference, in order to rest, but they had gone ahead and set up for me to preach on Sunday. So, things got started "right off the bat." I was the major speaker for one morning and two evening sessions in addition to two elective afternoon sessions. Youngmi was again our gracious host and drove us where we were needed to be. It was a very busy few days, and I experienced the most intense times in God that I have ever had. I pressed into Him continually that week and found myself in almost constant prayer. I felt His presence like never before and felt His overshadowing love. Donna and I had an interview with a Christian magazine, and as they would ask questions, I would literally break down in tears because of His love that I felt. God manifested himself with signs and wonders in every meeting. At the end of one morning session in the main auditorium, the Lord had me pray individually for every person in the audience who wanted prayer. As I walked down the aisle of people with the interpreter, many were spontaneously slain in the Spirit, healed, and set free without hands being laid on them. After that session, I only had forty-five minutes before the evening session, and as I walked down the hallway, people would again be slain in the Spirit for the anointing of God was so strong. The whole conference was like that. God's presence filled the room. A future student of the MEDTS, Youngmi (Rebecca) Ha, was at the meeting and gives a brief description.

Youngmi (Rebecca) Ha: The first meeting and first wave of the Holy Spirit occurred in my life. I met Don for the first time at the Inner Healing Conference (The Presence of the King) in Onnuri Community Church in Korea in 2013. At that time, I was a baby Christian and did not understand the Holy Spirit or the spiritual world. I just attended the conference without any hope and purpose. Don was one of the main speakers at this conference. In my memory, during the middle of the conference, he suddenly stopped his lecture and then started ordination prayer for every person according to the guidance of the Holy Spirit. When he put his hands on my head and prayed, I stared at his eyes and saw a big wave of the Holy Spirit coming in his eyes and coming toward me. The wave covered me, and then I fell back on the floor. It was a very mysterious experience for me. After finishing the conference, I forgot him and went back to my normal life. But I could never forget the blue waves from his eyes to me.

Don: We will hear more from Rebecca later as she testifies of her growth in the Lord during the MEDTS 2019. We were scheduled to fly out Sunday afternoon and planned to rest in the morning before leaving. I was notified on Saturday that was I scheduled to speak at two services on Sunday morning at a satellite Onnuri Church near the airport. I was exhausted on the flight back to Dallas and slept most of the way. I felt so fulfilled knowing that I was in the right place at the right time and called of God to be a vessel of His glory. I was overwhelmed with His grace and love. I must admit it seemed rather anticlimactic to be lecturing in physiology back in Tulsa a few days later. It was almost as if I had two roles in life.

CHAPTER 14

Recurrent Battle with Back Pain and *Visitation* of Jesus

A few days into the January semester of 2014 I had a tremendous pain in my thoracic area and was having difficulty walking long distances because of shooting pain down my legs. I went back to see the neurosurgeon who did an MRI, CT, and myelogram of my spine. The lumbar area indicated spinal stenosis and arthritic changes with bone spurs, but the thoracic area revealed significant spinal cord compression. The myelogram also showed obstruction at T12 and L2. I was scheduled for urgent surgery. After my myelogram and before surgery, I pressed into God and hoped for a supernatural healing. Then on two consecutive days I received an unexpected call. The first from my spiritual father, Ralph Wilkerson, who gave me a word that God still had more for me to do. The next day Loren Cunningham, the founder of YWAM, called and gave me the same word, that God still had more for me to do. Their words were essentially the same that I had received in Zurich on 15 May 2013 from

FOLLOWING THE *Anointing*: PART II

Andreas Keller of Stiftung Schleife on our way to outreach to the Kurdish area of Iraq.

On 8 January 2014 I went into surgery for the thoracic cord impingement. The surgeon did a laminectomy to relieve the pressure on the cord and found an anterior calcified spur like a spike compressing the cord to one-sixth normal size. He attempted to remove it, but on continuous monitoring of my lower-extremity nerve function, all motor activity (muscle innervation) of the left leg was lost. He stopped attempting to remove the bone spur, and most of the nerve function returned. I did well post-op with good pain relief but had some nerve damage (spinal cord injury) to the left leg. He told me that my condition should have paralyzed me from the waist down. It was hard to imagine that I had been climbing the mountains of Iraq a few months earlier. The grace of God abounds. In subsequent discussions about what to do about this calcified spur, any attempt to remove would require an incision through my chest to reach the spur since he could not approach it from the back. The success of this approach was marginal, and he would not recommend it. Nor did other Tulsa neurosurgeons in consultation.

I praised God for His grace and protection, and in March I was able to return to the MEDTS 2014 to teach for a week. I struggled in my conversations with God about how I could teach and minister healing if I walked with a limp due to the spinal cord injury. I **heard Him say, "I have used other people with a limp."** Walking with a cane, I witnessed God move in healing others through his crippled servant. Was this to be my thorn in the flesh? Out of our weakness He gets the Glory. For many years to come, I would have constant discomfort from the spasticity in my left leg as I would pray for others.

Recurrent Battle with Back Pain and *Visitation* of Jesus

> **2 Corinthians 12:7-9** Because of the surpassing greatness of the revelations, for this reason, to keep me from exalting myself, there was given me a thorn in the flesh, a messenger of Satan to torment me—to keep me from exalting myself! Concerning this I implored the Lord three times that it might leave me. And He has said to me, "**My grace is sufficient for you, for power is perfected in weakness.**" Most gladly, therefore, I will rather boast about my weaknesses, so that the power of Christ may dwell in me (bold emphasis is mine).

In addition to the thoracic problem, I still had the challenge of the arthritic changes in my lumbar region. I could only walk a short distance before having to rest from the pain in the legs. I continued with the outpatient spinal steroid injections and prayed for healing in the lumbar area where God had touched before. I was able to return to teaching and finished the semester but could not tolerate the pain any longer. In May 2014 I underwent extensive surgery on the spinal stenosis in my lumbar area to release the pressure from arthritic bone spurs pressing on the nerves from three-disc levels. Hardware was placed in the lumbar area to stabilize my back in order for the fusion to heal. The pain after surgery was intense, and I was very discouraged. I had believed Him for healing, but there I was after surgery. My mind was racing, and I asked myself – had my faith been lacking? I was in turmoil, I had seen God do so much, witnessed and felt His supernatural power, but there I was in pain. During the surgery they had to repair the covering of the spinal cord, fix a drain for the leakage of spinal fluid, and insert a drain for the incision, and I could never get comfortable. The spinal cord leakage continued into the third day and should have stopped by then. The neurosurgeon had my bed put in deep Trendelenburg position (foot of bed elevated with head down at a thirty-degree angle) in an attempt to take the pressure off the covering of the cord in order for it seal by itself. I was on completed bedrest, in pain,

FOLLOWING THE *Anointing*: PART II

uncomfortable in that position, and I literally reached my limit. I had seen God do so much, enough for a lifetime, and prayed that He would take me home. I was desperate, exhausted, and felt as if I was in a major battle against the spirit of infirmary that I could not fight any longer. As I was laying in desperation in my bed, all of a sudden, I felt like I was laying on a big bird that was flapping its wings under my shoulders. Then the whole hospital room was filled with a bright white light. I looked in the corner of my room, and **I saw Jesus Christ standing there surrounded by a blinding light.** The light was so intense, yet I was able to see His beautiful eyes that were so blue. Peace filled the room, pain left, and I heard Him say, **"You have more to accomplish for me."** I fell asleep and awoke the next morning. The spinal fluid drainage stopped, and I was discharged home to go through the long recuperative post-operative period. There is no doubt in my mind that Christ is with me now as I minister in His name, still with a limp. I feel his love and presence as never before and had a new resolve that the Lord had more for me to do. **Is the Holy Spirit speaking to you also, do you have more to do for Him?**

CHAPTER 15

Medical Discipleship Training School (MEDTS) Kona 2015-2017

I returned to teaching at TCC for the January and August semesters. It was good to be back to teaching and my strength was returning. The MEDTS was in April that year, so we returned to Kona to help with the school. Dr. Bob Doe was on staff as well while also establishing the urgent care clinic. He shares about his time with us.

Dr. Bob Doe: Dr. Tredway and his wife Donna have a unique presence-based healing and deliverance ministry that was developed in the years of connection with Ralph Wilkerson and Oral Roberts. The couple pairs Don's boldness with Donna's gentle quiet but powerful approach. The power of God flows through them to set captives free and bring physical, emotional, and spiritual healing.

FOLLOWING THE *Anointing*: PART II

The Lord has moved Don in and out of healthcare, teaching, administration, and business, giving him a strategic level view of the healthcare system and placing him in position to gather many and to influence the development of God's model of healthcare.

This wonderful couple are positioned in this season to anoint a generation of health workers with the spiritual DNA to transform the system of healthcare and thereby nations.

The time is now – may they be raised up to activate an army of prophetic healers.

Don: I returned to TCC for the fall semester and again began to have pain in the lumbar area of my back. Spiritual warfare continued. The X-rays indicated that the screws had come lose in the bone. I had to take a few weeks off from school for removal of the lumbar hardware the middle of September 2015. The fusion was solid, so I went back to work after a short time off. In addition, my left knee began to hurt. I had an arthroscopy and removal of a torn meniscus and was informed that I had little cartilage remaining in that knee.

Donna and I began preparing to go to the 2016 MEDTS that was to start in January. There had been a turnover of personnel on the base, and for the first time we had no one from our staff that was permanently stationed there who could monitor situations concerning our school. We found out in November that our school had not been listed on the English or Korean websites for the Kona base, and it was too late to rectify the situation. We ended up with only four students that we transferred to YWAM Ships, Kona, which had a medical stream in their DTS. It was very discouraging for us and the Thompsons. Donna flew to the island to help with the orientation of the students.

Medical Discipleship Training School (MEDTS) *Kona* 2015-2017

The Ships ministry, under the leadership of Brett and Karen Curtis, invited us to their base for the 2017 School. They and the administrative staff would take care of all the student applications and processing. All we would have to do is review the applications for acceptance when they were complete. This seemed an answer to prayer after our experience with the 2016 school at the main Kona base. Bruce and I talked to Loren Cunningham who agreed to let us move to Ships for 2017. It was at this time, too, that I felt the Lord was asking me to retire from TCC in order to devote my full time to the MEDTS and the opportunities He had waiting for us. Consequently, I retired at the end of the fall semester 2016 from TCC.

Medical Discipleship Training School (MEDTS) Kona 2017

MEDTS 2017 was an exciting class. This was to be our largest school, thirty-one students. Up until this time we had limited our students to health professionals or ones in training, and the ages were usually above twenty-four years old. Ships felt strongly that all ages should be admitted and required that of us. We had had a few younger ones at times but had not had a good experience. Consequently, this was quite a change for us. We now had to open the school not only to healthcare professionals or those in training, but to those who were interested in going into that area. As I prayed about the age challenge, I also felt the Lord convicting me of not fulfilling one of the YWAM values, "Championing Youth." I was excited about being at Ships after not having a DTS in 2016. I also had been asked to join the board for the Ships Ministry out of Kona and Orange County, California.

Claudia and Greg Burke were among the students who have stayed on as staff for several years. Below is their insight into the school.

FOLLOWING THE *Anointing*: PART II

Claudia and Greg Burke (MEDTS 2017- 2019): We did our DTS in 2017 at Ships campus. It was our first real exposure to YWAM culture, following a few months the year before working as Mission Builders. Although much of the information in the teachings was familiar, DTS has a unique way of connecting one's heart to the heart of God. Don, your precious sense of humor blended with a sound obedience to God's Word made each day a new encounter with God's delightful loving nature. I particularly enjoyed how you evoked facial expressions from Donna that said, "I can't believe he said that or did that." It spoke volumes about the strength of God's love in your marriage. You clearly love and appreciate each other's unique gifts, bending and swaying as the breath of God leads.

I was especially surprised when God knocked, ever so gently, on the door to my heart that winter. He had opened my heart to feel what He feels in the fall, before we came to the Medical DTS, preparing me for what He had planned in January 2017. The pain I sensed in Jesus's heart for other students and myself was overwhelming at times. I did not expect God to use His feelings to awaken the hidden feelings of rejection from my own childhood. DTS helped me start that journey of inner healing. Donna's wise coaxing and encouragement during our one-on-one sessions helped me recognize lies of the enemy that were hindering my true identity in Christ. There were many days that Donna's deep compassion was evident as I watched her hold weeping students in her arms. She allowed God to heal their hearts through her amazing strength and love. Her spirit sings like a Viking warrior, loud and clear, a strong tower with deep roots. I feel DTS, guided by both of your willingness to be obedient to God's leading, is what prepared us for an outreach experience with God that changed my life forever. I returned home, grounded like never before, with renewed determination to serve

Medical Discipleship Training School (MEDTS) *Kona* 2015-2017

God in whatever way He chooses to call us. Our home pastor called us "ruined for Jesus," and that is the truth.

Our continued involvement in the MEDTS under your mentorship has grown into a deep friendship, filled with respect and love for who God created you to be in His kingdom. When you teach, Don, your eyes literally dance with delight, and your exuberance is like a roaring lion that is tempered with the gentleness of the Lamb. You are particularly gifted with insight to the spiritual realm when dealing with difficult situations, which are common to the DTS. I watched a quiet humility bow to the Lord as He guided your decisions. We have learned so much and are deeply blessed by your friendship.

Don: I was accustomed to helping Bruce not only plan but also manage the finances. Unfortunately, at Ships our administrative program was changed, and we were not given access to the budget and school administrative functions for the quarter. While the administrative support was excellent for student acceptance before we came, the support was deficient after we arrived. Ships was running a general DTS during the same time as ours, and it became apparent that Ships leadership wanted to place the Medical DTS under the leadership of the other DTS. The administrative problems were surprising to me and how unresponsive the YWAM ships administrator was. Donna and I met with him and shared the initial mandate for the creation of the MEDTS and why we believed we needed to have a separate school. He told us in no uncertain terms that they wanted us to be a stream of the general DTS and have no separate identity. It was apparent that we could not remain at Ships for the next school. We would have to move back to the YWAM Kona base if the school was to continue as an individual school.

FOLLOWING THE *Anointing*: PART II

Bruce is a fantastic leader with abundant grace but has a hard time with conflicts. As we discussed the situation with the Thompsons, it was apparent that they were not wanting to continue in leadership of the school. Every year Barbara had found it difficult to return, and I had the sense that Bruce was struggling whether to step down. Another situation then arose in that Ships leadership listed their own Medical DTS for the next year on their website. It was not to be an independent Medical DTS like we had been running, but rather a stream from their general DTS.

In addition to the frustration about the school, I had quite a challenge during the second week. I had a release of group and individual prophecy and could sense God's presence strongly. I was so excited and believed that after stepping down from TCC, I was now being released by God. The next day Bruce came to me just before morning worship and said that leadership had come to him and asked him to speak to me. They were upset that they had been limited in their time of sharing because I had given a word that had delayed the schedule. Bruce told me not to prophecy anymore. How crushing that statement was and especially coming from Bruce. I had been so fulfilled in the Lord and now so low in my spirit. God, have I heard wrong from you? Donna was ready to go home. In addition to the struggles there, there were the usual struggles at home with our daughters that seemed to happen at the beginning of a school. I decided to fast and pray and not attend classes for the remainder of the week. I was very discouraged. The enemy again had attacked in ways that I would never have expected. Bruce came to me the next afternoon asking for forgiveness for the way he had given the message. I shared with him that I was fasting and asking the Lord whether Donna and I should leave. Donna continued going to class for the lectures while I stayed away. The Thompsons did not want us to leave.

One morning that week, the Lord prompted me to go to the main YWAM base and sit at the common meeting area coffee shop called the Banyan Tree. I went and set down, and an acquaintance from the church we attended, a former YWAMer, came by with her children. I had a word for her that I did not understand, but she thanked me, saying that it confirmed what the Lord had been speaking to her. She was excited, and so was I. The Lord was still with me. That week was very difficult but also one of tremendous revelation. Suddenly, the Lord spoke to me to go to the following scripture:

> **Hebrews 12:12-13** Therefore, strengthen the hands that are weak and the knees that are feeble, and make straight paths for your feet, so that the limb which is lame may not be put out of joint, but rather be healed.

So often we concentrate and interpret only on the part of scripture that we want to hear. I was excited thinking that that scripture was implying physical healing for my left leg and its neurological defects. However, I was to learn that the next few verses were the ones that God was emphasizing and testing me in.

> **Hebrews 12:14-15** Pursue peace with all men, and the sanctification without which no one will see the Lord. See to it that no one comes short of the grace of God; that no root of bitterness springing up causes trouble, and by it many become defiled.

The situation with Bruce, my precious friend, and the Ships leadership is what God was speaking about a root of bitterness. It was not hard to forgive my good friend and mentor, Bruce, but it was much harder to forgive the Ships leadership because of all that had

FOLLOWING THE *Anointing*: PART II

happened. (There continued to be challenges with that relationship over the next few years for which I was constantly tested.) I wanted to resign from their board, but God said no. As of this writing, seven years later I have resigned. **The enemy always attacks where you least expect it.** That week while I was challenged, God confirmed that He was with me. He again reminded me to speak only what He reveals and not to try to interpret any word. He also reminded me that He and His Word would be my defender, not me. A scripture that God gave me to hold on to is:

> **Philippines 3:14-15** I press on toward the goal for the prize of the upward call of God in Christ Jesus. Let us therefore, as many as are perfect, have this attitude; and if in anything you have a different attitude, God will reveal that also to you.

If I keep on pressing into to God, learning more of His character, if there is anything a blocking my walk with Him, He will reveal it at the appropriate time There is still much of God's character that I need to know.

> **Philippines 3:10-11** that I may know Him and the power of His resurrection and the fellowship of His sufferings, being conformed to His death; in order that I may attain to the resurrection from the dead.

This week was a very difficult week for me but also one of tremendous revelation. I returned the next week to the classroom and witnessed God do amazing things in the students' lives and even the staff. We had a challenging student that had not finished another DTS and had come to ours. Donna took her under her wing becoming her one-on-one staff. She would go on to finish after going on outreach with Donna to Iraq. As the Burkes have shared, we witnessed God doing major things in all the students' lives.

Medical Discipleship Training School (MEDTS) *Kona* 2015-2017

One of the lecturers for the school was Sarah Lanier[15]. She was, in fact, a senior person in YWAM and used by many bases for conflict resolution between cultures. Bruce and I sat down with her to discuss the future of the school. Bruce related that this was going to be his final school and asked what should he do with the school. Sarah advised that if he felt released of the burden and no new leader was apparent, then perhaps the time of the school was at an end. I shared with Donna after that meeting. Was God asking us to take up mantel for the next year? We had never considered leading. Bruce believed that we needed younger leadership, but Donna and I were in the same age range as the Thompsons – in our 70s. We prayed, and we felt the Lord was calling us to do so in order to bring up new leadership. Due to the situation at YWAM Ships and them advertising a Medical DTS of their own, we would have to return to the main Kona campus. Bruce and I met with Loren, who readily endorsed us returning to the base.

I asked in class during the last two weeks if any of the students wanted to return and join us as staff. God had told me to buy six Israel prayer shawls, and six students came forward after class indicating that they were interested. Four of these students would join us next January on staff.

Each year we had various popular outings from the school. The beach days and barbecues of course were very enjoyable. One good time was a Saturday tour around the island bus trip. We would hire a local tour bus and see the Island as a group. It was a wonderful time away from the classroom and had good interactions with our local bus guides. If we had extra seats, we would sell them to other YWAMers. This year a couple and their two young children from the Ships base accompanied us. They would join us the next year as staff. They had a young grade school daughter who enjoyed the trip so much that at the end of the long day when she was exciting the bus, she put her arms around the bus driver's neck, hugging him saying, "thank you, this has been the best day of my life." I witnessed tears running down the cheeks of the bus driver. **How the love of a small child can witness the love of the Lord Jesus Christ.** No wonder Christ said in

> Mark 10:14 …Permit the children to come to Me; do not hinder them; for the kingdom of God belongs to such as these.

Toward the end of the lecture phase, if a student wanted to be baptized in water for the first time or again as a commitment to the Lord, we would give them an opportunity to do so in Kailua bay. It was exciting to see the responses of people as they were baptized. We always had them to speak out why they were being baptized and any affirmation that they wanted to declare. Often through the different school leaders or pastors, specific prophetic words would be given to them. Each year it was a highlight of the school, but this year it was quite exceptional. Many staff from the Ships ministry witnessed the baptism, and even some of them were baptized also.

Water Baptism MEDTS, 2017.

Medical Discipleship Training School (MEDTS) *Kona* 2015-2017

With each school there was a "Love Feast" which is common in YWAM. This is a nice dinner at the conclusion of the lecture phase and again at the end of outreach. There was usually a presentation by the students about the school, often comical in nature, with worship led by the students, then the presentation of certificates of completion for the lecture, and then also the outreach phase with the appropriate University of the Nations credits. In our schools we finished with communion which the leader of the school would lead assisted by staff. With all the trials for me during the school, to see the changed lives was amazing and reaffirmed why we were there. After this night of celebration, the next few days were spent preparing to leave for outreach or returning home after outreach.

We returned home to Oklahoma after the lecture phase, and I saw the orthopedic surgeon for my right knee. He recommended a knee replacement. It would be scheduled for after our return from Kona and the teams' debriefing upon completion of the school's outreach phase.

Don: The process to move to the main Kona base had changed and was difficult. I had to apply and be approved to lead the next school even though Loren had approved it. The leadership of the base was now younger, and most did not know me. Bruce conveyed to me that some of the training committee had concerns about me being a leader since I had never led a school, and he had never named me a co-leader. Also, some who knew me from Ships felt that leading a school was not my gifting, although they had never been with us in any class settings. I was also praying again about stepping down from the Ships Board. When I went to share that with Ship's leadership, I was told exactly the same thing that I heard from the main base, that leading a school was not my gifting. Their advice was that we should stay under Ship's ministry. I felt this was an attack on my character. Even though Donna and I had confirmation from the Lord and Loren agreed, I was having to go through **Hebrews 12:14-15** again. The training committee wanted to interview me, but the meeting was scheduled a few days after I was to return to Oklahoma. I was scheduled to have my right knee examined for scheduling of a knee replacement in June. I could not miss the appointment if I wanted to be ready for the school in January 2018. Bruce agreed to attend the meeting for me. Donna was upset with the base as was I. We believed we had heard from the Lord, so we had to leave it in His hands.

Bruce met with the training team. One of the elders of the base, Danny Lehman, was at that meeting and knew Donna and my ministry. With Bruce and Danny supporting me, the training team approved our leadership for the next school and allowed us to start preparing and finalizing staff. The story that Danny tells about me is significant. He met me when I was ministering at the Honolulu YWAM base when he was the leader. Donna and the girls had left YWAM to return home to Oklahoma, but I had a teaching engagement at the Honolulu base before I headed back. I was bringing a few household items back with me to Oklahoma and one of them was a small black and white portable TV that we had used in the bedroom. I had wanted to sell it or give it away, but the Lord told me to take it with me. While teaching in Honolulu, the Lord told me to give the TV to Danny's young son. I spoke to Danny about it and could see that he had some reservations, but he accepted it. You see, Danny didn't want his family to have a television and had told his son that he couldn't have one. Unbeknownst to me, his son had been praying a long time for a TV. Receiving the small television was quite important in his son's early walk with the Lord and also gave Danny another glimpse of God's character. Consequently,

Medical Discipleship Training School (MEDTS) *Kona* 2015-2017

the training committee agreed to my leadership of the Medical DTS (MEDTS). More important, I knew in my heart that I was appointed by God to lead the MEDTS for 2018.

While Donna dealt with the applications for the school, I had a right knee replacement in middle of June 2017. Before surgery I had arranged all the speakers for the school and the Lord had blessed us with a wonderful staff. One of my initial prayers was that the Lord would provide the staff that he wanted instead of me pursuing one. He did just that by speaking to individuals to come. Bruce and Barbara had recommended Malsoon Park, my interpreter on multiple occasions, as co-leader. She agreed and was very helpful in corresponding with the Korean applicants.

CHAPTER 16

Medical Discipleship Training School (MEDTS) Kona 2018, 2019, and Korean DTS

There were twenty-eight students in the medical DTS for 2018 with half being a combination of Korean and American Koreans. The first two weeks were a challenge. Six Korean students were always late to class in the morning. It was noticed that as soon as class ended for the day, this group of six would gather and walk to town and stay out into the early morning visiting various bars. The ringleader was a Canadian Korean third-year dental student. His parents had filled out his YWAM application for him and sent him to YWAM in hopes that he would begin to walk with the Lord. We also found out that he had dropped out of dental school, was married, and had been calling his wife at her home in Canada. Nowhere in his application did it mention anything about dropping out of school or being married. When asked about his wife, he related that he had wanted to marry her and had taken her home to meet his parents. They rejected her and told him that she was not of the same status as the family. Unknown to his parents they married. He said that he wanted to remain in the DTS, but his behavior did not change. The Lord gave me a scripture prayed regarding him:

> **2 Thessalonians** 2:8 Then that lawless one will be revealed, whom the Lord will eliminate with the breath of His mouth and bring to an end by the appearance of His coming.

Based upon that word, we discharged him and sent him home. We also confronted his female American Korean college graduate who was his partner in going out and staying out late at night. She was not repentant even after counseling with staff leaders and we discharged her also. The day that she was to be escorted to the airport, she came to the class, and as she was saying goodbye, she repented and asked for forgiveness. We let her stay. It was exciting to see how the class responded to her. One of our students, who was a Korean female physician, came forward and gave the young lady a note (to this day we don't know what it said). All of this happened just before lunch break. At the break, the female physician then went to her dormitory room, laid down on her bed and died.

The application system for that year had been dramatically simplified by the younger leadership of the base. There were minimal medical questions or questions relating to past illnesses. The Korean female physician that died had been treated for ovarian cancer and had stopped chemotherapy. She had applied to the Medical DTS and had come on vacation with her sister and mother to Kona before the school started. We noticed that she was having a hard time breathing and had sent her to the base physician. We found out the severity of her illness the day before she died. She had

Medical Discipleship Training School (MEDTS)
Kona 2018, 2019, and *Korean* DTS

terminal cancer. Our impression was that she had come to Hawaii to die. All of this happened in the second week of the school. I called Loren Cunningham that day informing him of her death. He said, " Don, I am glad that it happened in your school and not in a school with a younger leader." A great deal of administrative time was required to resolve the issues of her death with the local officials, the Korean embassy, and the family in Korea. Needless to say, the medical history part of the application process was changed.

One of the physician's roommates then left the base the next week and returned home without telling us. She had been struggling and had been seen by several counselors on the base. All of this happened the first few weeks of the school. Fortunately, the school settled down, and we had a very good DTS. What a break-in period as a school leader.

One of the other students, Christie, was a volleyball Olympian from Australia that surprisingly ended up in the MEDTS that year. In December, before the start of school, I was at a base worship time, and the Lord gave me a word for a man and woman standing in front of me. I had never seen them before. Below, Christie will share her experience in the MEDTS. Please note the depth of inner healing that the Lord took her through.

Christie: (written in the Cook Island in August 2020 during the COVID-19 pandemic.) It was December 2017 that the soles of my feet first stepped in Kailua-Kona, Hawaii. I was there for a well-deserved break with a friend, feeling exhausted and burnt out from all the things I was doing in Sydney to forge my vision ahead. Upon arriving onto the big island, we settled into our hotel apartments, and to me it was just an ordinary holiday to refresh with tropical breezes, sun, sand, and rest. My plan was to enjoy a short break

FOLLOWING THE *Anointing*: PART II

and then return home to Australia to begin my Tokyo 2020 Olympics campaign to qualify to compete for Australia in Beach Volleyball. However, God had other plans.

Kristy, a former YWAM Medical DTS staff member, asked me if I would like to tour the YWAM base in Kona. I had never heard of YWAM, but I am always open to sight-seeing and went along. Kristy was sharing stories about her and her children's history with YWAM while we slowly began to walk from the flags past the cafe to the media room. I felt a delightful and peaceful feeling as I walked along, stunned by the beauty of the trees. Kristy was explaining how YWAM works, and at the time I was most interested in a degree, so I was hungry for the right degree, especially one from a Christian university. I was completely amazed that a system and place like this existed. I could not believe that the teachers do not get paid but pay their own way to teach. "Sorry, could you repeat that?" I just wanted to make sure I heard right. "So, a doctor who has already sacrificed so much will come and pay to teach here? WOW." God does exist.

We then made our way into the media room next to the library, and she asked some staff members if they could play an introduction video for me about YWAM. I remember already thinking of how I can make this happen, but as I was watching the video, I became absolutely convicted that I wanted to complete a DTS (Discipleship Training School). In order to do one of their university courses I had to complete a five-month DTS. However, there were many streams from which to choose, and although business, leadership, and sport-related ones stood out, it was the medical one for which I felt a prompting in my spirit. But having no medical background or former interest, I ignored the prompting, thinking – that's not me, and I am not a medical person. I left the media room that day sold out on the YWAM base. However, I was not sold out

Medical Discipleship Training School (MEDTS) *Kona* 2018, 2019, and *Korean* DTS

on the Medical DTS stream, and I initially signed up for a business and government-related one. It was not long after during a visit to a worship and praise evening that I was worshipping, and toward the end, I got a tap on my shoulder. I turned around and the man that I was standing in front of introduced himself as the Medical DTS leader Dr. Don Tredway. No way! I do not remember exactly what he said because I was caught off guard by his introduction of who he was. I was still getting promptings by the Holy Spirit about Medical DTS, but nothing was convicting me to change until that moment – exactly like I knew I had to be at YWAM. I knew in that moment that I had to be in the Medical DTS. Don and I would laugh later about how significant that tap on the shoulder was. Thank goodness Don was good at recognizing that prompting of the Holy Spirit.

In these deliberating days, I rang my son and his father, asking for their blessing for me to return in three weeks' time and explaining to them I would be away for five months. My son had never been without me this long, but a new stepmother had come into his life, and it seemed more possible as he had recently begun to live with his dad full time. They gave me their blessing, and it was one of the few green ticks I had to get for me to know it was confirmed by God as an open door. If I continually get resistance and everything is going wrong after praying, I usually see that as closed doors and God is protecting me and blocking me.

I filled out the application and sent it off. I required $4,000 for the five months, which was not payable until January 4th. My holiday in Hawaii came to an end. I left for Australia in December and packed up my entire unit, placed it all in storage, and prepared to leave in three weeks' time. My son was caring and understanding. I was very frustrated at this time that I was not seeing my son as much as I would have liked. The ex-husband complained I

FOLLOWING THE *Anointing*: PART II

was working too much, and I was. I was working all year building a cleaning business which required working to early hours in the morning. I was competing in the Australian Volleyball League and Sydney Volleyball League, taking up every Sunday and at minimum two evenings in the week. There was many events and public speaking engagements I had accepted throughout the year. I was a Pain Pod and One80tc Ambassador. I was running an anti-drug campaign with high profile athletes, and my body was working off five hours sleep.

Over three weeks in Sydney I had walked through and overcome all the blocks and passages you have to navigate with fast decision making and turnaround times for moves of God. I departed for Hawaii January 4, 2018, excited, scared, and hopeful for what lay ahead. It was a leap of faith into the unknown. I was seeking and searching for more of God. I was on fire for God and wanted to experience more of his divine presence and teachings. I went to Hawaii to rest and get straight back into it. That would not happen.

I was the first student to arrive at YWAM Kona. I was led to a dormitory of bunk beds to fit ten women, but as one of the eldest in this class I was moved and placed in a room of five single beds. I will always be thankful to Don Tredway for having the discernment to do so.

Over three months we sat in a classroom full time and learnt a subject over a week or two. The first week or two I was getting up before 6 a.m. as I always do to exercise down at the beach volleyball court down the steep hill in town from the YWAM base, fully expecting to compete in the world beach volleyball tour once this was done. However, I soon stopped all exercise and let go of Tokyo 2020 Olympics. I felt convicted by the Holy Spirit in class that

Medical Discipleship Training School (MEDTS)
Kona 2018, 2019, and *Korean* DTS

God was asking me to lay everything down and not for a time but forever. I was devastated and struggled with my flesh and mind to drop my last chance at competing in another Olympic games. It was the beginning of dying to self. I later heard that DTS (Discipleship Training School) is really known as "Die to Self." That made complete sense to me now. I began to see that the fairytale of following Jesus was something I had created in my mind but that the reality of it was in the Bible the whole time. Lose your life for God, leave family and all you are doing, and follow me. I was expecting to be trained in medical practices and Christian teachings, which we were, but most of the teachings brought on inner healing, healing which was limiting us in life. I remember describing it to someone as being in a hospital bed because I had no strength often to do anything after class but sleep due to the emotional toll it took on me facing traumas of the past. Slowly I let go of more, including Candifest Ministry, The Wander Organization, and public speaking. I deleted social media accounts, stopped exercising, and completely rested and gave away everything. I felt like a nun in a convent completely devoted to God in these days. I struggled the entire time to let go and rest. I felt real grief in these days. I was sorrowful and although I was happy to give away things in my life to have more of God, the process of letting go was uphill, and I had to fight with my flesh and pride. I prayed at the start to be more humble, and now God was answering my prayer. I thought to myself I will never pray that prayer again. I did continue to pray for humility, but the pride is not so thick these days, so the fall to drop to my knees is not as far as it first was. I had a dream that all these submarines were coming up to the surface from the deep sea, and I would find out later that these submarines were memories and trauma from the past that I needed to face. The Holy Spirit was the sun, and it was shining light on these submarines that broke the surface into my reality and awareness.

FOLLOWING THE *Anointing*: PART II

HEALING FROM NOT BEING ABLE TO REST

The greatest healing during this time would be learning to rest. Unbeknownst to me, there was an undercurrent pushing me at an extremely fast pace in all that I did that ran from childhood. It was a blind spot affecting my decision making, and it was a submarine coming to the surface.

During DTS a speaker was invited for each subject and the volunteer staff would sit in class with us to pray and help us with the course program and whatever God did in class each day. The staff are graduates of Medical DTS, so they know what to expect and what we are going through. Over the course of three months, all the students and staff become your family, and you form incredibly tight bonds with people as you share intimate details and walk in the path of vulnerability together. Like any iron sharpening experience, some might sharpen your tool kit while others rub against you the wrong way.

I do not recall which subject we were studying, but I remember Donna Tredway holding her hand on my heart, and with my eyes closed I felt the fire of the Holy Spirit go through her hands and like an X-ray machine reveal what was within my heart bringing to mind a distinctive memory. I was in year three, and I won gold in the 100 m all the way to NSW state level. I was always winning everything to do with sports at a young age, and I assumed this race would be no different. I placed fifth in the heat, and I walked off the track crying to my parents who were there watching. I had run bare feet all the way to state level, but we were told shoes would have to be worn. I blamed the shoes and was devastated that I lost. I was back to the moment of defeat, and Donna was guiding me with questions. By this stage I am deep in the memory with my eyes closed feeling all the emotions like I am right there. That is the point. The Holy Spirit will bring up a memory and take you back as if you are at that point in time again. By losing that race I was always behind in second place and always wanting to win and be first, never achieving it no matter what I did achieve from that point on. That showed up in my life by being competitive in everything I did and always wanting to get to the top in everything I did. I had the mentality "sleep when you are dead," and I was ruthless and often reckless with no limits in all that I did. I would go to any extreme to get what I wanted, but as soon as the goal was achieved, I would still feel in second place, unsatisfied, and would find the next race and goal to win. Donna led me into where Jesus was taking me, what he was doing and what he was saying. Jesus took me back into the memory and helped me to finish the race. I cried tears of release and relief. In that moment I felt every kilometer and all the coal I had burnt on top of me as weight disappear. People used to tell me to slow down, and it was abnormal how much I did. They were tired and dizzy watching me. I could see and feel that. By finishing the race that day, I was able to stop sprinting a 100 m race in life and start to see life as a marathon. This was a significant first step in healing my unhealthy drive to achieve, win, and compete. There was still further healing to come from a performance spirit and critical spirit in future classes, which also would help to heal my inability to rest.

HEALING FROM FEAR OF FAILURE

I always thought that I was fearless and strong. As an Olympic athlete you would not think of fear as being a part of your life. However, I was to find out that it was. Dr. Don Tredway was standing in the front of the class and rubbing his stomach one afternoon, asking if anyone had a pain or trouble in their stomach. I would always touch my stomach, and the Holy Spirit was prompting me before with my stomach being an area of concern. As soon as Don asked the question, I lifted my hand convicted that it was me, and I wanted answers. By this stage the healing process was very familiar and for me, it was another submarine coming to the surface affecting my life that needed to be healed. I was shocked when a memory came to me in class. I was recalling how we were hit as children and there was nothing wrong with it as I believed in the island culture that hitting's were normal. Yet as I began to talk about the hitting's, I began to cry. When prompted how I felt, I was fearful and scared to make mistakes, because I was fearful of getting a hitting. This had instilled a spirit of fear within me. When I was taken back into the memory of the childhood house in which I grew up, I was asked what Jesus was doing when I was getting hit. Jesus showed himself comforting me, and then when I asked for Jesus to go into the memory, I could see the house and everything on the land being burnt down. Then I was seeing a beautiful green forest and trees growing tall everywhere, and Jesus was there smiling. I had pure joy as the memories where I was hit was now replaced with Jesus smiling amongst trees. Climbing trees as a kid was my favorite thing to do.

Don: What Christie shares above is very typical of what God will do in your life if you submit to Him. I know that I myself had to go through "a dying of self" in order for God to move in my life just as Christie shared above. Is God beckoning you to come to know Him in a deeper way in order to fulfill His call on your life? **His love and knowing His character better will change your life.**

> **1 Corinthians 13:7 (AMP)** Love bears all things [regardless of what comes], believes all things [looking for the best in each one], hopes all

Medical Discipleship Training School (MEDTS)
Kona 2018, 2019, and *Korean* DTS

things [remaining steadfast during difficult times], endures all things [without weakening].

Our four outreaches for the 2018 school were two teams to Papua New Guinea (one to the Highlands, the other to YWAM Ships/Highlands), one team to Thailand, and another to the Amazon in Brazil. The Lord spoke to me to do a pastoral visit to the Highlands when both teams would be there. Medically I was still recovering from my knee replacement and had started having trouble with my left knee along with the difficulty of the spinal cord injury. I knew that Papua New Guinea would be a challenge but also knew that God wanted me to go. In faith I went on that outreach. I did fine both on the plane and in Papua New Guinea. It sounds strange, but in addition to traveling mercy, I prayed for a western toilet and decent bed. God blessed us with both. A brother of one of the staff at YWAM Ships had opened a new motel near the airport. I was accommodated there along with the two teams. I was able to meet with the director of the local hospital and from that, a MOU (memorandum of understanding) was developed that would be important for future outreaches.

In addition to the Papua New Guinea teams, the Amazon team had a good outreach except for the staff leader who became ill and had to be hospitalized and treated in Brazil. Christie shares how this difficulty was turned to a blessing.

Christie: The single most important lesson I learnt from my Medical DTS outreach in the Amazon Jungle was that my identity was in Christ. The first jungle outreach started off with our leader becoming ill and needing to get back to the YWAM base asap. Suddenly and unexpectedly, we were left without a leader and having to decide on what to do in the jungle with our local hosts and translator. We decided to pray about it. Upon praying about it, we were led by the Holy Spirit on what to do next, and after seeing the success in direction as a team, we continued to pray until we returned to base camp. It was a highly successful first jungle outreach due to prayer. There was no leader required among us as we were all leaders following one leader – Jesus Christ. As long as we continued to seek Christ, we would know what to do, and it would all be ok. This was the first lesson of many to come – that my identity was in Christ.

Don: That summer we received an invitation to speak to a Korean summer camp in Kona. I spoke on the Family of God and the Trinity and Donna on generational sins and the way it has affected our family. It was a special time, and God moved in wonderful ways.

After returning home to Oklahoma, the knee pain returned, and I had another total left knee replacement in August 2018. More surgery, more pain, and more physical therapy. We then began preparing for the 2019 school.

In late November 2018, we were invited back to lecture in the major Korean DTS on the Kona base. Donna was not able to go. It was the first ministry opportunity after the knee replacement, and I found it rather challenging, but God was faithful. Many were touched that week. Was God finally opening up the doors again for ministry after so many years? In many ways I felt that I had been kept in a closet while I practiced medicine.

During the 2017 MEDTS, one student stood out who was a trauma nurse. She joined our staff for the 2018 school, and I felt that the Lord was calling her, along with our lead interpreter, to be co-leaders for the 2019 school. Many speakers had commented on the leadership abilities of the nurse, and I sensed that she eventually

Medical Discipleship Training School (MEDTS) *Kona* 2018, 2019, and *Korean* DTS

could become the leader of the school. I had let her organize and run the weekly medical lecture series in the school. She was very capable and did a good job although she tended to be very independent at times. She became my right hand in many administrative tasks as was our lead interpreter with the Koreans. I did not see it at the time, but major conflicts would arise between the two of them.

Once again, I believed the Lord to provide an excellent staff for the upcoming school. He did just that. One of the couples on our team was Ticee and Rob Graham from Alaska. Rob was a paramedic fireman and quite an evangelist. They lived next to the Denali National Park in Alaska and had an outreach ministry to the native Eskimos of Alaska. They were an answer to prayer. For several years one of the outreaches that was on my heart to establish was to Native Americans. I had tried several times to develop one to the Iroquois in New York, but it had never materialized. The Grahams would take an outreach to Alaska to minister to the natives there. God at times never works the way you expect.

Medical Discipleship Training School (MEDTS) Kona 2019 (Intense Struggles and Last School in Leadership)

Twenty-six students appeared in January with only three Koreans. It was a difficult class and presented many challenges, especially with a Korean couple who were there on the verge of a divorce seeking reconciliation. In general, the students were quite young and rather immature. Donna and I were more like grandparents and felt at times a little out of touch with them. Some of the students were challenged early in the school in regard to the release of the Holy Spirit in their lives, and many had no understanding of the Holy Spirit whatsoever. That all would change by the end of the lecture phase. It was wonderful to watch the transformation.

FOLLOWING THE *Anointing*: PART II

That quarter we also had a week sharing with another Korean DTS and also a combined Primary Health Care and Counseling school. During the week with the Primary Health Care and Counseling School, I was sharing on the Holy Spirit when all of a sudden, the Lord stopped me and began to give me a word for various people. He had me go to one young lady and start stroking her hair and say that that was like what her grandmother did in the past. She broke down crying and the Lord began healing her of deep hurts as she was held by a staff member on her lap. It is hard to describe how you feel when you see the depth that God goes to bring freedom. Thank you, Father, for allowing me to witness Your Glory. You did come to set the captives free.

> **Luke 4:18-19** The Spirit of the Lord is upon Me, Because He anointed Me to preach the gospel to the poor. He has sent Me to proclaim release to the captives, and recovery of sight to the blind, To set free those who are oppressed, To proclaim the favorable year of the Lord.

There was more conflict in the school. This time with some of the staff. One of our translators was very perceptive and came to me with a grieving heart saying that she felt there was disunity in the staff. Indeed, there was. Bitterness and resentment developed, especially with our Korean staff, over certain issues with the nurse co-leader and discipline relating to a Korean couple that were having marital difficulties. I thought the difficulty with our nurse co-leader at the time was mainly due to cultural differences. Staff meetings became verbal dumping grounds instead of constructive criticism. In addition, open conflicts developed between my two co-leaders. The nurse said she wasn't sure if she would come back for another school, while the Korean co-leader committed to another school only if Donna and I were the leaders.

Medical Discipleship Training School (MEDTS)
Kona 2018, 2019, and *Korean* DTS

Later in the quarter the nurse co-leader and another school leader related that after much prayer they felt that the nurse was to lead the next DTS. In spite of the conflicts with the Korean co-leader, I was pleased because I had sensed that she would eventually lead the school. I asked the nurse if she would be comfortable leading a bilingual school which she said she had no problem doing. The other school leader then had her kneel before me and asked me to pray and release the school to her. I was surprised, but I did it without taking it to the Lord for confirmation. The next week was one of emotional turmoil for me. I had difficulty sleeping and also was attacked by the enemy during the night. I had intended to go one more year, but now I was stepping down. I now realize that I was premature in releasing the school as I had felt the Lord had told me that we were to lead for three years. That would mean one more year.

Shortly afterward, on a Saturday morning, the school leader invited Donna and I for brunch to discuss the transition with her and the nurse. I was really troubled in my spirit as we met. The leader shared that we were the old wine skins, and it was time for us to step down and for the new generation to take over. I felt that I was being pressured by a matriarchal type of spirit. I shared that she and the Korean co-leader would have to work together, and she related that the Korean would have to understand that she was the leader. It also troubled me more that both she and the school leader did not agree to the concept of my mentoring during the next school year. The statement about being old wine skin hurt.

Donna was relieved to be released, but it was very difficult for me. I recognized that I had gotten myself into a situation by releasing the nurse co-leader too soon. That next morning as I prayed and pressed in about my concerns, I believed the Lord said to my mind,

"Do you trust me with the nurse?" I then felt the burden of leadership lift although I still had concerns.

All of this was taking place as we prepared for Love Feast at the end of the lecture, and the troubled young Korean couple came to me and asked to have a rededication marriage ceremony during the Love Feast. I was excited because I thought that God had moved in their hearts although Donna was doubtful while the Korean co-leader and I were encouraged. After the Love Feast, the next few days are always busy as people prepare to go on outreach. An older staff member had become close friends with the nurse co-leader, becoming almost a mother figure for her. Both had requested that they do the pastor visits for all three teams (Alaska, Thailand, and Peru). Donna, the Korean co-leader, and I had no reservations, so I agreed although I was troubled in my spirit.

The next few weeks I counseled with both co-leaders individually as well as together. It was apparent there would be difficulties in working together. The nurse still felt that she had to be in charge which was not acceptable to the other. My Korean co-leader would only stay if Donna and I remained. I then talked to an elder of the base about the nurse assuming leadership, and he said there would be no problem as long as I recommended her. I had a hesitation in proceeding, yet I believed in my heart that the Lord had spoken to me to step down and appoint her. I would have to submit a recommendation to the training committee who approved and appointed DTS leaders.

More conflict with staff: A couple of weeks before outreach, I learned that one of our Korean staff members who was scheduled to be on the outreach team to Alaska had been secretly corresponding with a doctor in Anchorage and had met him when he had come on

Medical Discipleship Training School (MEDTS)
Kona 2018, 2019, and *Korean* DTS

vacation in Kona. Her motives were questionable as her religious visa was about to expire and she would have to leave the country after outreach unless she had could find a sponsor for a green card. I questioned her about her motive of wanting to be on the Alaska team, and she responded that she was not even sure that she would see him there. More to come later.

Donna left for home a week before me. I finished up all the administrative issues at the end of the school. Just before the teams left for their outreaches, a couple on our staff opened their home for a final good by potluck dinner. One of the senior Korean couples on staff and two other Korean staff members came to me before the dinner and pleaded for me not to step down from leadership, saying that they would help recruit more Koreans for the next school. It was apparent that the school would not continue as bilingual with the nurse in leadership. I did not share with them that I had heard from the Lord but said I would continue pray about it, which I did. I had also been asked by another staff to confirm the nurse as the new leader at the staff potluck. I went before the Lord again and heard the same thing, "Did I trust Him with Emily?" At the close of the evening, the staff shared individually. One senior Korean staff person shared how much she enjoyed the school and how she had seen me grow in leadership over the years. At the end of the sharing, I announced that I was stepping down and had recommended the nurse to head the next school. I had been parked next to the elder Korean couple that complemented me earlier that evening, but now they would not talk to me. I returned home to Oklahoma with a heavy heart, later to return at the end of May for outreach debriefing.

At home the difficulty sleeping continued with tremendous grieving in my heart. Donna felt that I just couldn't let go of the school, but my heart and spirit were troubled. I felt that I had

FOLLOWING THE *Anointing*: PART II

somehow missed the Lord. I heard nothing from the training committee at the Kona base about the nurse being approved for the next school even though I had sent additional emails asking if there was a problem. I received no response. The whole situation troubled me. It reminded me of times when I was chairman of the department when I struggled with administrative decisions that I had to make after major conflicts involving personnel. I now realize that I was fighting against a Jezebel spirit from my past.[16,17]

Continued problems on outreach: As noted previously, the nurse co-leader and the older staff person did the pastoral visits to all three teams. During this visit the Peruvian team expressed that there were conflicts within the staff. Some stated that all the time was spent doing clinics but none in intercessions and spiritual warfare. Consequently, there was a division in the loyalty of the students to various staff members. I was told that the issues were worked through although more had to be done during the week of debriefing.

During the pastoral visit to the Alaskan team, they called me to say that the Korean staff individual had left the team to do to prayer walk in Anchorage, spent time with her boyfriend, and became engaged. On Facebook there was a notice from her fiancé that they were going to be married at the end of outreach. What a surprise. The outreach leader also called me to say that she had not been leading the team as was her responsibility but was preoccupied with her pending marriage. She was also disobedient in not following rules which were set about women running alone in the mornings. Alcoholism was common in the Indian villages, and she was putting herself in danger because of a high rate of being raped. She also informed me that she was not planning to return to Kona but go to Anchorage at the end of outreach for the wedding. It was

Medical Discipleship Training School (MEDTS)
Kona 2018, 2019, and *Korean* DTS

recommended that she be relieved of her staff responsibilities. She was.

The last pastoral visit was to the Thailand team. The nurse called to inform me that the Korean couple was not doing good. The wife had separated herself from the team and would only occasionally go with her husband to the outreach clinics and then just sat by his side. The wife of outreach leader was her one-on-one, and the doctor's wife refused to talk to her. She also had lost weight and there was concern about her physical status. There had been concern at the beginning of the outreach about her, and I corresponded with the leader about the importance of documentation and the process of how to send someone home. Her husband was doing good, but nothing had been dealt with regarding his wife. I shared my concern about her physical status and recommended that she be evaluated medically. The nurse co-leader recommended that she be sent home from the outreach. There were only three weeks left in the outreach, but Donna and I felt she needed a medical evaluation and should leave the team for that evaluation. I talked to the husband personally about my medical concerns and requested that they return to Kona for evaluation, but they elected to return to Korea. The whole process was difficult for them and the team. I received a note from the husband that they had returned safely to Korea. He would not correspond with me afterward, and I subsequently was informed that her medical exam was normal. There was more to come. I now see the trail of discontent and broken live that followed the nurse co-leader.

The two co-leaders had done the planning for the week of debriefing and did an excellent job, indicating that they could work together. It went extremely well and showed me how they could work together if they chose to do so. During that week, I was summoned

FOLLOWING THE *Anointing*: PART II

before the head of the training committee regarding the dismissal of the Korean couple. Complaints had been received by the base leadership from the Korean couple, my senior Korean staff, and surprisingly from my Korean co-leader. She was upset that she was not involved in the decision to send the couple home. She had sent the complaint before she had discussed the situation with the nurse co-leader, Donna, and me. I felt betrayed. The nurse co-leader and I met with the Training Leader and an elder of the base to explain the situation regarding the Korean couple. It was a difficult meeting, but the elder concurred with the decision, although questioned whether the couple should have gone on outreach at all.

There was a foot washing for the students by the staff on the last day of student debriefing. The elder Korean staff couple were the only ones not to come. It was a precious time, and the Lord would give us a word for the students as we washed their feet. The nurse co-leader and Donna did one group of students while the Korean co-leader and I did the others. The Korean co-leader asked me to wash her feet at the end of the service. There was healing and a deep sense of God's presence.

The next morning was staff debriefing and a final staff lunch that I sponsored. The meeting was the most volatile staff meeting that I have ever attended. Most of the staff were uplifting except when it became the time for the elder Korean couple to share. They were very bitter as to how the situations were handled both with the Korean couple and the Korean staff person in Alaska. The Lord spoke to me that morning to be humble. I asked for forgiveness in the way things were handled but not in the decision and regretted not involving the Korean co-leader. They were very bitter and accused me of being a racist. We all went to lunch afterward, but everything was superficial.

Medical Discipleship Training School (MEDTS) *Kona* 2018, 2019, and *Korean* DTS

The training committee had still not approved the nurse's leadership for the next year. I had to meet again with the base training leader who had arranged an afternoon meeting with Loren Cunningham and her regarding the change in leadership that would result in the school not being bilingual since the Koreans refused to work with the nurse. That morning, I had been asked to speak in the Word Alive DTS and experienced a wonderful move of God. The school was under the leadership of Jackson Ndecheck, a young man from Africa that God released as an evangelist in Cameroon. The Lord had me share on struggles in our identity with Christ, and I did so from a hurting heart. I shared some of my struggles with health issues and how the Lord ministers to us through our weakness. All of a sudden, the presence of the Lord filled the room. He gave me words for various individuals that touched them and caused them to break down in tears as God ministered to them. It continued for a couple of hours, and I had to leave for my meeting with Loren Cunningham. The Lord's presence stayed in that room for the rest of the day. There were no classes that afternoon. The students just remained in the presence of God. What a privilege to see God minister to His people.

I anticipated another difficult meeting with the base training leadership and Loren, but I had just left God's presence in the classroom, so I knew He was with me. I shared with Loren that when we started the Medical DTS, it was intended for Korean physicians who were retiring. I had reviewed all the Korean participants of the DTS since 2012 and noted that we had not had any Korean physicians that had recently retired. Yes, God had ministered in the school over the years, but I felt we needed a new avenue to reach the intended group such as a one to two-week seminar in Kona and even in Korea. I also shared with Loren what the Lord had spoken to me and that

FOLLOWING THE *Anointing*: PART II

I felt the anointing lift as leader for the school. I believe the base training leader was surprised that Loren agreed with me and felt the school should go with the nurse as leader and not be bilingual. He said he wanted Dr. Thompson and I involved as speakers in the Medical DTS and also involved in seminars. He wanted me to be a mentor for the nurse leader during the next school and specifically stated that he did not want me doing the planning for the seminars. After that meeting the nurse was affirmed as the 2020 leader for the MEDTS. I shared with the nurse the result of the meeting and that the training leader would be meeting with her to convey what Loren had instructed. I subsequently found out that the training leader never met with her, which I believe contributed to a strained relationship between the two of us and my non-involvement with the next school.

Also, in an attempt to help the nurse, I supported the appointment of Rob Graham, a fireman paramedic from Alaska, as co-leader of the next school. I still left with a broken heart about the whole situation of the DTS and the change in leadership, not really having peace. As I mentioned before, I believe I released the nurse into leadership too soon without asking for confirmation from the Lord. Donna and I should have remained in leadership for another year, fulfilling the three years that I felt the Lord had originally spoken. In preparation for the next years MEDTS, the nurse was the quarter-point DTS person (overall DTS administrator) for the next quarter and took the YWAM leadership course to prepare for the leadership of the Medical DTS. I was hopeful that she would succeed in leadership of the MEDTS.

Even with all the personal struggles, the Holy Spirit was ministering in a powerful way to the school. Rebecca shared earlier about

Medical Discipleship Training School (MEDTS)
Kona 2018, 2019, and *Korean* DTS

the ministry at Onnuri Church. She now completes her story since she was a student at that school. I am also including what she shared earlier for the completeness of her story.

Youngmi (Rebecca) Ha MEDTS 2019 (written during the COVID-19 pandemic): There is one personal thing I asked Don about writing his book. As people read the book, I hope that your readers will know that God is alive and that God is love. Also, to the readers, don't focus on just the story of Don and Donna's ministry but their life. Just as the Jesus who appeared on the road to Emmaus continued to walk, I hope this book will contain a life that bears witness to Jesus who accompanied and led their lives. I remembered Don's first lecture to us in DTS, and at that time he quoted the story on the road to Emmaus (**Luke 24:13-35**). Even now I remembered the preaching from this verse. I love it.

I know Don is known to many people as the Medical DTS Leadership and as a competent and renowned intrinsic healing instructor. However, I hope that the other side of this book will tell the story of the fragile times Don and Donna had, making mistakes and fears. I always remember the fullness of their love and prayer to students and staff in my mind. I thank them for their love, prayer, and humility in my Medical DTS.

Now, the whole world is suffering from coronavirus pandemic. I believe this is also a situation God has allowed. However, after this corona virus pandemic, the world will enter a time that requires a completely different way of life. While I am completely alone here in Jerusalem, Israel, God continues to show and speak to me how different the next world will be than before. It is my transforming season. It's a thankful time.

FOLLOWING THE *Anointing*: PART II

1. The first meeting and first wave of the Holy Spirit in my life

   I met him, Don, for the first time at the Inner Healing Conference (the presence of the King) of the Onnuri Community Church in Korea in 2013. At that time, I was a baby Christian and did not understand the Holy Spirit or the spiritual world. I just attended the conference without any hope and purpose. Don was one of the main speakers at this conference. In my memory, in the middle of the conference, suddenly he stopped his lecture and then started ordination prayer for every person according to the guidance of the Holy Spirit. When he put his hands on my head and prayed, I stared at his eyes and saw a big wave of the Holy Spirit coming in his eyes and coming toward me. The wave covered me, and then I fell back on the floor. It was a very mysterious experience for me. After finishing the conference, I forgot him and returned to my normal life. As one thing, I could never forget the blue waves from his eyes to me.

2. The second wave and joining YWAM

   In May 2018, I had a mysterious dream. In my dream, I was lying on a mountainside and looking down, and people were skating and playing on the frozen sea below it. Then suddenly the frozen sea surface was broken, and a very large wave poured over it and completely overwhelmed me on the mountain. I was completely sucked into the waves. After waking up, I couldn't sleep any longer because my dream was so vivid and inspired. At that time, I was working in a Christian NGO to serve NK refuges, and many staff members in my organization were YWAMers. In addition, I didn't know much about YWAM at that time, but since August, I started

Medical Discipleship Training School (MEDTS)
Kona 2018, 2019, and *Korean* DTS

wanting to be a YWAM missionary. Finally, I was looking for a DTS at the Kona Base around October, and I found out that Don was the leader of the Medical DTS. Without any hesitation, I applied for Medical DTS, and in my mind, I wanted to meet Don and his wife Donna again. If I say one more thing, I believed the first wave was connected with the second wave in my dream, and God was calling me to Kona. God was speaking through my dreams.[1]

3. The Big waves in Kona, Hawaii

On January 3rd, 2019, I arrived in Kona, Hawaii to do Medical DTS. There I met Don and Donna again as well as other wonderful YWAM missionaries and lovely colleagues. There were not only big waves rising from the sea every day but also big waves of young people gathered at the Kona base to follow Jesus. One feature of 2019 Medical DTS was that unlike other years there were many students in their teens and early twenties. For this reason, many students had not recovered from the inner wounds and pains from their families and communities. Although we were a medical DTS with a lot of medical personnel, the time was given to heal these wounds and pains more than other DTSs. This was done through internal healing in each week's curriculum and the plumb line ministry of Bruce and Barbara Thompson which specialized in this area. Our leadership, Don and Donna, and staff continued to worship and prayed for the recovery of young people. In particular, Don and Donna loved the students and

---

1 Matthew 2:12, 13a, NIV, "And having been warned in a dream not to go back to Herod, they returned to their country by another route. When they had gone, an angel of the Lord appeared to Joseph in a dream."

prayed for them with the hearts of grandfather and grandmother, or father and mother.

4. Fear and prayer

To be honest, in the beginning of DTS, I was afraid in my heart. It was rising up from many reasons since English is not my first language, I was much older than the other students, and there were only a few Asians with completely different cultures. Nothing could lighten my mind, and I kept my fears in my mind. Without anyone knowing it, I was an army officer in the past, so I looked like I was very brave and extravagant in appearance, but it was fake. I prayed to overcome my anxiety and fear. Don seemed to know it because every time he met me; he prayed for my fear to disappear.

In Corporate week's Thursday gathering, Don prayed for me, and at the same time I felt very strong touching of the Holy Spirit.[2] And then I could not move and was like a snowman for a long time, but my fear was burned out and disappeared. I shouted, "I am free, and my fear does not belong to me any longer!" I jumped and praised. It was an awesome moment in my DTS.[3]

---

2   Acts 2:38, NIV "Peter replied, "Repent and be baptized, every one of you, in the name of Jesus Christ for the forgiveness of your sins. And you will receive the gift of the Holy Spirit."

3   1 John 4:18, NIV "There is no fear in love. But perfect love drives out fear, because fear has to do with punishment. The one who fears is not made perfect in love."

Medical Discipleship Training School (MEDTS) *Kona* 2018, 2019, and *Korean* DTS

5. Tears' Maundy

   The most memorable moment of my DTS is the Maundy we had the day before our graduation. In the debriefing season after finishing our outreach, I was a little depressed for several reasons. A few students were struggling with what happened during the outreach period, and I also felt uncomfortable because the Korean couple did not finish outreach and went to Korea first. I thought it would be better not to express this, so it was more difficult to pretend to not be uncomfortable. Finally, Don and Donna apologized to the students on behalf of leadership and then washed the feet of all our students one by one. At this time, all students continued crying as the two of them washed students' feet and prayed with all their heart and mind. Everyone was weeping. But all of us could feel their love and sincerity and humility. I could feel what is true leadership. Therefore, I wanted to learn the leadership of YWAM, and then I was asked as staff to attend the biblical leadership school in Kona. Don and Donna are not perfect leadership, but they are an honest and humble leadership with lots of love. I was so happy and thankful that you guys were my leadership.

6. Love and encouragement

   When I started living as a staff member, Don told me many times, "I am so proud of you that you are joining the staff." His encouragement and prayer were so powerful for me. Those had helped me to serve sincerely as a staff in the hot summer season in Kona. After finishing serving as staff, I went back to Korea to meet my family and took a rest. And then I left for Herrnhut in Germany to do a second

FOLLOWING THE *Anointing*: PART II

SOW (School of Worship). I am so grateful that I have my wonderful leadership that supports me no matter what I do and no matter where I live. There is no fear in me because of the love of God, my loving parents, my supporters, and the leadership of Don and Donna. And one more thing, when I was in trouble in my outreach, Paraguay, I sometimes read Don's message sent on the last day of last year, "May I always be on the lookout so that I shall not miss a single one of Your great surprises. Amen."

Staff and Speaker Geoff Jackson MEDTS, 2019.

Don: Before I left Kona, I called the elder staff Korean man in the school and asked to get together with him and his wife to share with them their concerns about the Korean couple and the staff person on the Alaska team. He was very angry and told me they would never meet with me. I was heartbroken. When I left to go home after all that had happened, I was exhausted and had difficulty sleeping for the next month. I was grieving.

It also became apparent that the new leader of the MEDTS did not want me involved with the next school. I wanted to teach a week as usual but was not invited, and she would not answer my emails. Passwords were changed, I had no access to the applicants, and

Medical Discipleship Training School (MEDTS)
Kona 2018, 2019, and *Korean* DTS

there was no mentoring as Loren had directed nor advice sought. I felt very dishonored and found out later that she had thought that I didn't trust her. She had misunderstood when I shared what the Lord had asked me about not trusting God with her. I tried to explain what the word meant, but I am not sure she received it. The Grahams were co-leaders, but I was not involved in the school. There again, with the Koreans and with the MEDTS's new leader, I was walking through the scriptures in Hebrews that the Lord gave me in 2017.

> **Hebrews 12:12-15** Therefore, strengthen the hands that are weak and the knees that are feeble, and make straight paths for your feet, so that the limb which is lame may not be put out of joint, but rather be healed. **Pursue peace with all men, and the sanctification without which no one will see the Lord. See to it that no one comes short of the grace of God; that no root of bitterness springing up causes trouble, and by it many become defiled;** (bold emphasis mine)

I was identifying with Jesus in a different painful way, being misunderstood. God also showed me that this was an attack of the enemy attempting to destroy the ministry He had given me, especially to Koreans and those of Asian descent. His grace allowed me to turn the other cheek while the spirit of man in me did not like doing it.

> **Matthew 5:38-39** You have heard that it was said, "An eye for an eye, and a tooth for a tooth." But I say to you, do not resist an evil person; but whoever slaps you on your right cheek, turn the other to him also.

Perhaps God is speaking to you now as you read the grieving from the depths of my heart. If so, He will use it to produce growth in Him. Even after forgiveness, it may take a while to heal the

wound of the hurts, but God is faithful. Pray and ask for his grace to walk with you during this time of your life. Let his love flow from you.

As Loren had directed, the training leader and the leadership of the base decided to have seminars for Korean medical people. When I wrote to the training leader about the status of the seminars, I received no response. Unfortunately for me, the Korean seminars were to be managed by my disgruntled Korean staff person. Others were invited to help and teach. Even though Loren had instructed that I be involved to teach, I was excluded. I have had to stand against any bitterness in my heart, forgive those by whom I have felt offended, and believe God for restitution. Father, help me fulfill this scripture.

> **1 Peter 3:9** not returning evil for evil or insult for insult but giving a blessing instead; for you were called for the very purpose that you might inherit a blessing.

The Lord began speaking to me about persecution in identification with Him. One morning in my morning devotional, the topic was from

> **John 15:18** If the world hates you, keep in mind that it hated me first.

Looking back, I realize that I was wrestling with a Jezebel spirit[16,17] during that episode. I had not recognized it at the time, nor taken authority over it. That spirit's scheme is to destroy the priesthood of God, relationships, and the works of God. The power of God defeats that that Jezebel spirit.

> **I Kings 21:23** Of Jezebel also has the LORD spoken, saying, "The dogs will eat Jezebel in the district of Jezreel."

Medical Discipleship Training School (MEDTS)
Kona 2018, 2019, and *Korean* DTS

God used the different situations in the school and the struggles with the transition to grow in Him. I realized that academic reputation and integrity had always been an important part of my life. I had seen the results of others who were not truthful in the area of science and how it affected their professional life when the truth was discovered. The enemy came after my professional reputation through legal trials, as I shared before, but he didn't win. Then the attack came from where I least expected it, through the school and the transition, to try again to destroy my spiritual (priest) reputation. My devotional again spoke to me through

> **Matthew 5:10 (MSG)** You're blessed when your commitment to God provokes persecution.

My relief came as I went deeper in trusting God and believed that all relationships will be restored. His battle is His and not mine. I need to be aware of the schemes of the enemy and stand in the authority that God has given me. I have to be sure that bitterness does not get ahold of me, pray for those who speak ill of me, and trust that God will vindicate one day. **Are you walking through a similar situation? Do not let a root of bitterness fill your life. Seek the Lord and learn to rejoice in Him even in your time of persecution and being misunderstood.**

During the next two years Donna and our former staff in Alaska would begin to exchange email updates, and eventually I would meet with that person and her husband in Kona for a healing of relationships. **As I forgave, the Holy Spirit moved in the hearts of others.**

The Lord had other plans for me when I was not invited back to speak in the Kona MEDTS. I received an invitation in February to teach for two weeks at the Perth, Australia YWAM base. We had wonderful times with the students and fulfilling times of ministry. We stayed on for several more weeks and visited friends in various parts of the country.

At home, I began to have increased neck pain and balance issues. The cervical fusion that had been done years earlier had not fused cervical discs four and five. The neck pain and shoulder muscle spasms increased to the point that I had another cervical fusion with internal fixation August 2019.

I was invited to a University of the Nations College of Counseling and Health Care (YWAM) meeting in Chatel, Switzerland five weeks postoperatively. My physician gave me the OK to go with certain conditions, and Donna accompanied me. The meeting was concerning the Health Care and Counseling sections of the university that had been under discussion for several years, and it was important that I be there. The flight to Switzerland was a challenge, and I could never have made it without Donna. The meeting was good, as well as seeing friends, but it was also one of continued grieving for me concerning the school. God was good, however, and for while at Chatel there were students from past schools, and I heard of others, who God had continued to bless and launch into ministries. I thank God for showing me all that had been done over the years, but I was uncertain of what my future involvement would be.

Donna and I stayed a couple days longer at a hotel in Geneva. It was relaxing to spend time again in Geneva where I had worked so long. We enjoyed the few days together visiting our old restaurants and relaxing after the Chatel meeting. The biotech company for whom I worked had closed the corporate biological division office

Medical Discipleship Training School (MEDTS) *Kona* 2018, 2019, and *Korean* DTS

in Geneva and moved it to the main office in Darmstadt, Germany. What was my future with YWAM Kona? Donna wanted to sell the condo in Kona.

Korean DTS 2019

At the end of November, I was invited to speak at another Korean DTS about the character of God. I had thought that my ministry in Kona with the Koreans had been compromised. It wasn't. As I shared on the Character of God in relation to the Trinity, the Lord would have me stop and give words to individuals as I lectured and ministered. It was a wonderful time.

During this week, the Korean interpreter Jimmie was touch by God. We ministered on generational sins and then went into an individual prayer time for those that responded. It was a class of approximately thirty staff and students. I began praying on one side, and the Lord instructed me to have Jimmie pray on the other side. I never will forget his face when the anointing of God went through his hands as he prayed for a student who was slain in the Spirit. You are never the same after God uses you in ministry. Thank you, God, for your faithfulness. It was a glorious week. I was invited to return next year another Korean DTS. God is faithful. I was so fearful that I had failed Him and others during the Medical DTS, but He was still with me, and His anointing remains. I was invited to return next year to two Korean DTSs. **God is faithful. Are you concerned that you have missed Him? If so, talk to Him. He is always available.**

Romans 11:29 for the gifts and the calling of God are irrevocable.

Other things were happening in 2019 along with the conflicts of the school. A year and a half earlier we expanded the Urgent Care

FOLLOWING THE *Anointing*: PART II

Clinic to the Kalihi area of Honolulu. We had a local launch team who had obtained significant backing from local churches, but we could never get local providers to enter the picture of whole person health. We also had subleased a clinic from another organization and found out that we had signed an unfavorable contract. We had many board meetings during this time and eventually had to close the Honolulu clinic. I went over to Honolulu after the closing of the clinic to attend a Sunday service at Kalihi Union Church where they honored the clinic and believed that God would one day raise it again in order to help the underserved.

I met an interesting lady at the church. Her son had worked at the clinic, was excited about whole person medicine, and was now premed in college. She came to Kona the next weekend and spent the next three days in a school where I was teaching and recorded the teaching. I taught on the Character of God through the Trinity, and once again God's presence filled the classroom and touched His people, including this lady. The Lord had her there so that she could have an encounter with Him!

CHAPTER 17

Medical Discipleship Training School (MEDTS) Kona 2020 (Time of Grieving) and Trip to Australia February 2020

Staff training began for the 2020 MEDTS in January. It had been a tradition since the start of the MEDTS to do the training at the Kailua Military Camp at the volcano on the Big Island. It is a beautiful place for a retreat, and being retired military, I was able to use the facility. The new school leader asked me to continue the tradition for that year. I would make reservations and partially support the retreat. Either Donna or I would be required to check the group into the camp. I went, checked them into the camp, and intended to leave, but the new leader asked me to wait until everyone had arrived.

FOLLOWING THE *Anointing*: PART II

There had been some healing between the leader and me, but I still felt some reserve from her. She never asked for my advice about anything in regard to the school, nor was I invited to speak that year. Donna felt this was just confirmation that we were finished with the school and Kona. I was still grieving over the whole situation, but the Lord said just to be humble and let no root of bitterness take hold. Before I left, to my surprise, the leader and staff had a prayer time for me and thanked the Lord for all that I had done for the medical DTS. I still remembered the phrase, "You are old wine skin," but I tried to let it go. I left Hawaii and returned home to Oklahoma and prepared for our February trip to Australia.

My annual visit to the urologist revealed that my PSA (measure of the prostate gland hormonal level) was quite elevated. An MRI had revealed a suspicious area, and the urologist was insistent upon doing a perineal biopsy. It was done in the Oklahoma Surgical Hospital, formerly the City of Faith Hospital, in the same room where I had done gynecological surgery. Donna thought it was God's humor. A week before we were to leave for Australia, the biopsy report came back positive for early prostate cancer. Another battle. God, when will it stop? I prayed and felt the Lord say go on the trip, and the urologist agreed. The scripture that came to mind was:

> **James 5:16** Therefore, confess your sins to one another, and pray for one another so that you may be healed. The effective prayer of a righteous man can accomplish much.

The portion "pray for one another that you may be healed" seemed to jump off the page to me. As I would pray for others and confess my sins then I may be healed. I went on the trip believing God for healing.

Medical Discipleship Training School (MEDTS) *Kona* 2020 (Time of Grieving) and Trip to *Australia* February 2020

Trip to Australia 2020

We flew Cathay Pacific through Hong Kong on the way to Perth during the beginning of COVID-19 in China. It was good to fellowship again with friends in Perth. The first week was the Primary Health Care School. The first day the Lord changed what I was going to speak on and had me speak on the mother heart of God. There was a mighty move of God, especially with one Asian girl who had never known her mother's love. God presence filled the room as we watched God work. The Lord again used Donna to minister. The week was exciting as we continued to share on the character of God through the Trinity. We had two weeks at Perth YWAM separated by one week.

During the week between, we traveled about 260 miles south of Perth to Albany to visit a pastor who we met on a previous trip to Australia. I felt the Lord say that he needed encouragement. He had arranged for us to do a weeklong conference of teachings and drove to Perth to take us to his city. It was a good time of reconnecting and fellowship. The pastor explained that he had had some major surgery, and during his time of recovery, the church had dwindled to just a few people. He apologized for the expected small numbers to attend the meetings even though he had advertised locally. The Lord had us reassure him that the size of the meeting didn't matter, and we had come because God had told to us to in order to encourage him and to remind him that God loved him. The average size of the meetings on Sunday and the rest were four to five people as well as God presence. We had a blessed, restful, and peaceful time and enjoyed the beautiful scenery of Western Australia.

The second week in Perth was with the Medical Missions class. The students came from a very traditional background, so we continued speaking about the Holy Spirit. One morning we had the opportunity to speak in another class, and as we started to speak, the Holy Spirit filled the room. He made His presence known. Soon almost all the students were on the floor experiencing the touch of God.

One afternoon at lunch, the base leader's wife mentioned that she was to speak that week at the Thursday evening community meeting but couldn't get confirmation from the Lord. She asked if I would pray about speaking. Donna and I looked at one another because on the bus trip from Albany to Perth, we both had sensed that we would be ministering at that meeting. The Lord later that day confirmed that I was to speak and gave me an interesting passage:

> **Hebrews 1:7 and 13-14** And of the Angels He says, "Who makes His angels winds, and His Ministers a flame of fire.........But to which of the angels has He ever said, "Sit at My right hand, until I make thine enemies a footstool for thy feet"? Are they not all ministering spirits, sent out to render service for the sake of those who will inherit salvation?

I asked God to honor His word and to release His ministering angles that night during the meeting. At the meeting He gave me some words of knowledge had me share a little about a young lady who had gone to have an abortion and how the Lord intervened. God then had me ask those to whom He was speaking to come forward, and Donna would pray for them. There were probably about 300 to 400 people in the meeting, and at least a hundred came forward. Donna looked at me saying, "help," and I asked the leaders to help us pray. Worship continued, and God came in power releasing His anointing through all the leaders. People came forward seeking His presence, and the meeting continued until around one in the morning. The leader of the base said that he saw angels on each side of the stage that night. Kathryn, the leader of the Medical Missions class, comments on the meeting.

Kathryn Kennedy: It was an amazing time of ministry, and such a great move of God and His presence. All this before the COVID-19 came, and to think that it was the last thing that people remember before they had to leave, is so good.

Don: From Perth we flew to Sydney where Christie, one of our students from the 2018 MEDTS, met us and the next day drove us to Canberra to spend to spend several days with Tom and Dianne Hallas. Tom was head of YWAM Australia, and what precious hosts and a joy to be around they were. We rejoiced over the times that the Lord had given us in the past and talked about the future. He wanted us to come back and spend time with the YWAM bases in Australia. God what are you saying? It was a wonderful time visiting and seeing the sights around beautiful Canberra. I had an opportunity to speak at the YWAM base the last night before Christie came to take us back to Sydney where we met our friends, Dr. Ernest and Lynne Crocker. We spent a day with them, where we visited by a mutual friend, David Grantham. We also met their friend Jason before they took us to the airport. Ern tells a little about that day.

Dr. Ernest Crocker: During your recent trip to Sydney, I invited you to pray for my dentist pal. He was an evangelical Anglican, thirsty and searching for the Spirit of God. He was a driven man, often referring to himself as a "human doing" rather than a "human being." But all his striving had simply made him exhausted, frustrated, and the target of many who wished to take advantage of him. I met with him for lunch on the Friday before you came to stay. We talked and I prayed for him. The next morning you guys and

FOLLOWING THE *Anointing*: PART II

David met with him at our home and prayed for him. Your words for him were "rest" and "wait." The next day a friend who had led our team to Cambodia a few years before also prayed for him. On that same day Lynne was browsing in Sascha's room (our daughter) when a book at the back of the bookcase caught her eye. It was *You Shall Receive Power* by Derek Prince. She placed it beside her bed. On the Tuesday morning, she had an overwhelming prompting from God to send the book to Jason that day. So, we drove to his surgery and hand-delivered it together with a note from Lynne. Unbeknown to Lynne, Jason's wife had also written to him on that same Tuesday, and her words enforced what Lynne had written, to rest and wait. Jason began to read the book on the Tuesday and finished it on the Saturday. The final chapter contained the words "waiting on God changes us." He is a changed man.

> **Isaiah 64:4** For from days of old they have not heard or perceived by ear, Nor has the eye seen a God besides You, Who acts in behalf of the one who waits for Him.

CHAPTER 18

Prostate Cancer and COVID-19 and The *Prayer* of Caleb

Don: We returned home the first of March just before the COVID-19 pandemic began. We were unable to travel and remained home in Broken Arrow where I began writing the first draft of our journey with God. I returned to my urologist who rechecked my PSA. It was still highly elevated, so we went through the treatment options. I had believed God for healing and how I had wanted the supernatural. I had his promise and had to walk out how He was going to heal me. Radiation therapy was recommended, and I had peace about it. It consisted of forty treatments, five days a week. It started out fine in the beginning, but toward the end the fatigue was extreme, and I had a hard time doing anything. At times I even felt as if I was dying. I trusted God and desperately wanted Him to touch me. A few months after finishing the radiation therapy, my blood PSAs started to slowly decrease over two years until it was in normal range. God healed through medicine. Again, I had to walk out what I had preached for Him.

I had been scheduled to return to Kona during May and June for teaching sessions in the Korean DTSs, but the COVID-19 resulted in the schools being cancelled. One morning I joined a Kona staff meeting by Zoom from Oklahoma. One of the items for prayer was a YWAMer named Do Lai. I had heard of him. He was from Miramar and had helped arrange some major YWAM outreaches to his country. He was severely ill with COVID and was hospitalized in Tulsa. His wife and children were in Tulsa and were part of the Miramar community. Do Lai was in an ICU on a ventilator, and his wife was unable to see him. The base was asking for prayer for him and his wife. His wife, Kim, was quite fearful since English was her second language. The Lord gave me a burden for him. I was able to obtain his contact information from a base leader and contacted his wife. With her permission, I was able to contact his doctor and check on his daily status. His wife and I texted often updating her on his situation. It is interesting that his doctor was the son of a colleague from my ORU days that I remembered as a small boy. For the next month his status remained critical, and he was transferred to another hospital for ECMO. This is a machine used for heart surgery bypassing the lungs. The blood is diverted into a machine for oxygenation. Do's lungs had such an inflammatory reaction that he was not oxygenating his blood satisfactorily. Other patients at this stage of the disease would be on ECMO for a few weeks. As the Kona base, myself, his family, and the worldwide community of YWAM interceded for him, he was only on the ECMO machine for two days. He rapidly improved and was discharged home in a couple weeks. He, of course, had extensive physical therapy after that. What a miracle, God had intervened!

Prostate Cancer and COVID-19 and The *Prayer* of Caleb

I "just happened" to be in Tulsa when I usually would have been traveling if not for the COVID-19 pandemic. God is in charge even during a pandemic. He even gave me more opportunities to teach by Zoom during that time.

God also reminded me of the word that He gave me when I retired. It was that I would not be traveling as much but would be more established with people coming to me. I found myself becoming involved with multiple organizations at the board level. I was chairman of the board of a non-profit organization, Blessing International, a company providing medicine for missions. This was established by a pharmacologist friend, Harold, who had been at ORU with me in the early days. He had shared his vision with me, and I had seen the business grow from his garage in the '80s to that of a large organization. Harold had retired and new leadership had taken over. Harold had called me in 2013 while in Kona and asked me to come on board during the transition time. With my industry and mission experience, I can now see how the Lord had prepared me for that.

In 2017 I was asked to serve on the board of YWAM Ships. I have seen God do miraculous things through that ministry. Even though I wanted to come off the board due to situations occurring at the 2017 MEDTS, the Lord said stay. I have been blessed to see how Bret and Karen, leaders of YWAM Ships, have faithfully followed God in this ministry. To believe God for the ships to serve the waterways of the Pacific and South America has been a challenge and a witness for me. It is a privilege to watch them in action.

While being involved in the MEDTS in Kona, I was also on the board of the Condominium Association for Hualalai Village, the place where I said that I would never live. I served for about five years, the last couple of years as Chairman. The Village association consists of two factions, condos owned by individuals and those by the University in which a lease hold arrangement exists. Due to the financial difficulties in the beginning and the long time it took to complete the project, there was some animosity between the early owners and the later, especially the university. I had to be a peacemaker and help work through the situation. Finally, the Lord let me off the board after five years, and when I left the relationship was much better.

I was also on that board of trustees at the church I attended in Kona and would occasionally preach on Sunday mornings and also helped work through various conflicts within the church.

In addition, I was also chairman of the board for Transformation Health Network, which was the parent board for Aloha clinic, the urgent care clinic in Kona Hawaii. I had seen that clinic as the seed for whole person health that the Lord wanted to establish in Hawaii.

The Prayer of Caleb

As I am writing this story, God reminded me of a word given to me in the '80s that I would be an administrator, which I did not receive at the time. As I look back and long for being able to share the gospel and minister in meetings as like I used to, I know physically that I cannot. I am still believing for **Hebrews 12:12-13** that my weakened and lame limb will be healed as I work to fulfill also **verses 14 and 15** of not becoming bitter and being at peace with all men. Writing this story, I realize all of the boards that I am involved in now is a lot of administrative work. Is this the fulfilling of the word given to me years ago? I wonder if there is someone else reading this that you came to this same realization? It is so easy to recall and live in the past and not recognize the way you are being used now, one that you could not have imagined. With maturity in God, our roles change. At age eighty-two in my current medical condition, I am praying for Caleb's strength for I still have mountains to claim in His name.

> **Joshua 14:10-11 (MSG)** Now look at me: God has kept me alive, as he promised. It is now forty-five years since God spoke this word to Moses, years in which Israel wandered in the wilderness. And here I am today, eighty-five years old! I'm as strong as I was the day Moses sent me out. I'm as strong as ever in battle, whether coming or going.

As long as I am here on earth, I still have things to accomplish for God, fulfilling

> **Psalm 92:14-15** They will still yield fruit in old age; They shall be full of sap and very green, To declare that the LORD is upright; He is my rock, and there is no unrighteousness in Him.

CHAPTER 19

Aloha *Kona* Urgent Care Clinic (AKUC) and Medical Discipleship Training School (MEDTS) *Kona* 2021

We had a consultant and possible practice manager come to the clinic during the COVID time. I had planned to go and help orient him but was unable to book a flight to Kona due to COVID restrictions. He wrote a report to the board which noted significant leadership problems at the clinic and brought to light personnel and management issues which seemed to be related to the CEO's leadership. I needed to investigate and look at the situation. Donna had been very insistent that it was time for me to apply some of my administrative experience. As I prayed, the Lord spoke to me about being a peacemaker.

FOLLOWING THE *Anointing*: PART II

Matthew 5:9 Blessed are the peacemakers, for they shall be called sons of God.

At the direction of the board, I went back to Kona to investigate and interview the staff and appraise the situation. This was a stressful time. The CEO/medical director was having difficulties in his relationships with colleagues and employees. The consultant had given a very negative report regarding his management and interpersonal skills. He had recommended his immediate removal. I felt the Lord told me to be a buffer for him but also to help him work through his responses to people and work on healing of relationships. I was also amazed that most contracts, especially with providers, were verbal and not written. There was very little administrative structure, the one administrative person was overworked, and the CEO was very impulsive in his leadership. His relationship with others was devasting and a poor witness for Christ. At times he could be very spiritual, prophetic, and insightful praying for patients, but the fruit of the Spirit was not evident. He was a very good friend, like a spiritual son, and it was difficult trying to help him work through these difficulties. I worked with him for the next six months regarding administrative matters and started looking for a practice manager. As I tried administratively to bring order into the business, he and I were often in conflict. I reported my findings to the board and agreed to stay on working with the management team and the CEO as we looked for an administrator. The CEO would try to improve, but under pressure he would interact very poorly with co-workers. He wanted help administratively, but he could not accept it, always having to be in charge. Through an interviewing process we finally found and hired a chief operating officer who would report to the CEO and the board. We established written contracts with the employers, and I tried to work with the

CEO and the COO to establish procedures. As soon as I left Kona, the CEO reverted to his old habits, refused to change, and tried to control the new COO. I realized then he was blind in the areas that needed change.

It was also felt that the clinic was at a place in time where it needed to expand its services to full family practice in addition to urgent care, and more outreach into the community with social work, mental health, and addiction services in order to fulfill the vision for the clinic. We needed more full-time people in addition to part-time employees. It was also evident that in order to do that, we would need to transition the CEO from being the medical director and release him to other areas. I called an emergency board meeting recommending that he be released from day-to-day operations as medical director and reevaluate his role as CEO. The next few years were ones of turmoil as we tried to realign the clinic and reestablish the foundation. Unfortunately, after the 10th year anniversary we are faced with closing the clinic due to financial instability. However, as I am writing, another Christian organization has approached the board about assuming the liabilities of the clinic and continuing the clinic's whole person ministry. Hopefully the Lord is answering our prayers. If not now, He will bring it to pass with others.

Medical Discipleship Training School (MEDTS) Kona 2021

While in Kona and working at the clinic, Donna and I received an invitation to teach at the Medical DTS now under Rob and Ticee's leadership. Rob asked us to teach on the Ministry of Jesus in addition to Curses and Generational Sins. What a precious time we had in the Lord as He set His people free and revealed His character to them. We also were contacted by the elder Korean couple who had opposed us during the 2019 DTS, and they invited us for dinner. We spent a precious time together and had a healing of relationships. What a good God we serve who answers prayers. That was a great burden that was lifted from me.

Since the end of the 2019 MEDTS, I continued to question my decision to turn the school over to the nurse. I visited Kona a few years later in 2023 and learned from Rob that the nurse leader had left the 2020 school before it was finished. He and his wife then took over the leadership and have led that since that time. The nurse returned in 2021 for a portion of the school but again left not fulfilling her requirements. When I heard that, I was convicted again of acting impulsively by appointing her too soon. I asked for forgiveness from the Lord and finally was able to forgive her. The Lord had saved His school.

The Holy Spirit taught me to prayerfully consider all decisions. **God also showed me that many will receive opportunities, but not all will arise to the occasion.** I now see that this whole situation was the enemy's attack to destroy the MEDTS and our outreach to the Koreans.

Matthew 22:14 For many are called, but few are chosen.

During that trip I also felt that something broke in the spiritual realm for me when I finally forgave myself for missing the Lord. When I returned home to Oklahoma, I received a package from a dear physician friend in San Diego, California who also prays for his patients. It was a facsimile of the Purple Heart Military award. My friend had added the following note dated 21 March 2023:

Dear Don, I felt impressed by the Lord to order you this facsimile of a Purple Heart in July 2019. I was not released to give it to you until today. It symbolizes Bravery and the Heart of the Father. It also is a badge of honor for those who have served in the military and have sacrificed. I honor you and give this to you in a prophetic act and out of obedience to my daddy God. With Love, signed with his name.

The Lord had impressed upon my friend to buy this for me during the time I was struggling with the change in leadership in 2019, but he was not released to give it to me until four years later when, with a broken heart, I was able to ask for forgiveness, had reconciled with those involved, and forgave myself. **I have to ask myself at this point, could some of my suffering during this time be due to a lack of forgiveness on my part?**

We will miss God at times, but as we recognize it and in humility ask for forgiveness, attempt to reconcile with those involved, and forgive ourselves (hard for me, took four years), God will extend His grace to us. I now know His love at a deeper level. This Purple Heart award now sets in my office reminding me of how wounded we can become, and also of the loving heart of the Father. **Is God speaking to you now? Have you been wounded in His service? Ask the Lord to help you forgive others and yourself. Though wounded, wear the Purple Heart of the Father as a symbol of bravery, and walk through Psalm 23.**

CHAPTER 20

The Continuing Battle with Infirmary, Heal Me Lord

I had to return to Tulsa for an appointment with my neurologist who noted my increased difficulty in walking and referred me to another neurosurgeon with specialized training in spine surgery. The spasticity had increased in my left leg to the point I had to have Botox injections to control it. I had a repeat MRI, CT scan, and myelogram which indicated increased compression of the spinal cord from the calcified bone spur at thoracic spine level T11-12. The radiologist and other physicians were amazed that I could even walk. There was a new procedure to remove a bone spur in the area where mine was. It would require removing part of a rib on both sides of the vertebra and going lateral through the vertebra from the back to remove the spur without collapsing the lung (surgery previously for a bone spur of this kind would require going through the chest cavity and having to temporarily collapse the lung). The local neurosurgeon felt he could not do the new procedure but

FOLLOWING THE *Anointing*: PART II

referred me to a neurosurgical center in Phoenix, Arizona at the Barrow Brain and Spine Center. I consulted with the Phoenix physician who had developed the procedure and was told that bone spurs in the thoracic area of the spinal column were not a common condition and that he only did ten to twelve of these thoracic cases a year. Upon review of my file, he stated that my spur was the worst case that he had ever seen and would be at least a six-hour operation with a ten percent chance of being paralyzed. He also told me I had a cervical (neck) spur which also would need to be done at a later time. On top of that, my orthopedic surgeon said that I needed to have a shoulder replacement. That week was not a good week. I had been fighting pain in my back for eight years, praying and believing for healing, and now was told that I needed three surgeries. My primary care physician and neurologist felt that I had no choice but to go to Phoenix for surgery. My gait and difficulty in walking were getting worse. Upon sharing and asking for prayer from Christian friends, I received the following email from our good friends Dr. Bruce and Barbara Thompson:

Dr. Bruce and Barbara Thompson: Dear Don and Donna, we have been praying regarding your possible surgery plans. We sensed from some scriptures for you to proceed with both the cervical and thoracic procedures in faith and trust in Father. He hasn't healed supernaturally and so to proceed with prayer and naturally in surgery, seemed to be what Father was encouraging. Here are some scriptures we had for you to ponder:

> **Psalm 22:19-24** A messianic psalm relating to Jesus Suffering and then an expression of faith and hope toward Father. Praise Him, Honor Him, He has not ignored the suffering or turned His back on them. He has listened to their cries for help. I will praise you and fulfill my vows in the Presence.

The Continuing *Battle* with Infirmary, Heal Me Lord

Psalm 23 All especially His promise to protect and keep you by His goodness and unfailing Love.

Psalm 56:9-11 God is on your side. Trust in Him and don't be afraid. What can a mortal do to me (without God's permission). A sacrifice of thanksgiving in faith. You kept my feet so I can walk.

We submit these thoughts to you as you pray and seek His face for whatever He gives you a peace over! You continue on in our hearts and in our prayers.

— *Bruce and Barbara*

Don: There is no doubt in my mind that the Lord's purpose in having me write our story and to watch the old video tapes was to prepare me for the surgery that was coming. He reminded me of all the things I had seen Him do, His promises to Donna and me, and that He was not through with me for I had more to do for Him. Psalm 56 that Bruce received from the Lord really spoke to me since it was similar to a scripture that the Lord had given me a year earlier.

Hebrews 12:12-13 Therefore, strengthen the hands that are weak and the knees that are feeble, and make straight paths for your feet, so that the limb which is lame may not be put out of joint, but rather be healed.

This was the confirmation of the means by which God was going to heal me. This was to be my eighth surgery on my back. It was a such a spiritual battle especially after God had healed me of the failed surgery in 1977 when I was in the Navy.[1]

Donna and I flew to Phoenix and went to the Barrow's Neurological Institute for surgery on the 4th of August 2021. The

FOLLOWING THE *Anointing*: PART II

first week was a blur, I woke up in ICU after an eight-hour procedure. As I was waking up and before I opened my eyes, I heard the sound of the birds singing and literally thought that I had died and was in heaven. I then opened my eyes only to see and hear a nature scene with birds singing on a TV screen.

The surgeon told Donna that my case was the worst he had ever done. He had to remove one-third of my ribs on both sides at their T12 insertion, drilled out thirty percent of the involved vertebra in order to approach, and drilled out most of the spur while operating under a microscope. He had to leave some of the spur because of all the scar tissue with entrapped nerves. It was a very complicated surgery that also involved opening the covering of the spinal cord to dissect out the cord and nerves from scar tissue, laminectomies, fusions, and insertion of rods and screws for stabilization of the back. I lost a lot of blood and was transfused with three units of blood and one platelet pack.

When I woke up in the ICU, the pain was intense. I had never had pain like that and there were terrible spasms of the left leg. Every few hours the nursing staff would come in to check if I could move my legs. I could barely move the left one. The surgeon was pleased that I could even move my leg at all and said that it would take six to twelve months to determine how much function would return. I was also put in a back brace to protect the spinal fusion and would have to wear it for the next twelve weeks when out of bed. My post-operative course was stormy. In addition to the pain, I had drug reactions as they adjusted my medications. I reacted with not being able to think clearly and with vivid nightmares. The enemy brought up old fears at night from my time in Viet Nam War and tried to convince me that I was losing my mind. He would also bring to mind buried memories of traumatic experiences accusing me of letting people

The Continuing *Battle* with Infirmary, Heal Me Lord

down and being a failure. I now know torments of hell – pain, fear, and accusation with no relief, just despair. The prayers of those interceding for me during that time was very important, and I came to a new understanding of the intercession of Christ. He was with me in my pit of despair!

> **2 Timothy 2:13** If we are faithless, He remains faithful, for He cannot deny Himself.

The Holy Spirit brought to mind meaningful scriptures that He had given me in the past, and I began speaking them out loud to counter the lies of the enemy.

> **Proverbs 4:20-22** My son, give attention to my words; Incline your ear to my sayings. Do not let them depart from your sight; Keep them in the midst of your heart. For they are life to those who find them and health to all their body.

> **2 Timothy 1:7** For God has not given us a spirit of timidity, but of power and love and discipline (sound mind).

One of the ways the enemy works is to prey on our weaknesses. I was weak both physically and emotionally. I quoted the above scriptures again and again as the attacks came. **This time the enemy was trying to destroy my identity from within.** Donna was there to pray and encourage me. I was in the main hospital for one week and then sent to the inpatient rehab hospital for three weeks to undergo intensive physical and occupational therapy. I was evaluated by a psychologist with different tests who encouraged me that I was just undergoing drug reactions and was not losing my mind. One night while I was sleeping, the enemy again brought up the same junk from the past and also tried to convince me that I was paralyzed and would not walk again. I started speaking Hebrews 12:12-13 out loud and saying, "I can lift my leg." I began lifting both legs shouting that I could lift my legs and began shaking the side rails of the bed, making a lot of noise. A nurse from another ward was walking by my room and came in and asked, "Dr. Tredway, what is going on?" I felt alone and in despair. The nurse held my hand. Once she held my hand, I felt the peace God fill my body, and then she gave me a hug which filled me more with His presence. All the fear left my body, and I was at peace. This scripture came to mind.

> **Hebrews 13:5** ...for He Himself has said, "I will never desert you nor will I ever forsake you," so that we can confidently say, "The Lord is my Helper, I will not be afraid. what shall man do to me?"

Later that same night, the charge nurse for the next shift also came in and just held my hand. Again, I felt such peace. Thank you, Father, for using your servants to minister into the depth of my physical and spiritual being. Psalm 91 became a reality in my life especially the following verses.

> **Psalm 91:1-2** He who dwells in the shelter of the Most High Will abide in the shadow of the Almighty. I will say to the LORD, "My refuge and my fortress, my God, in whom I trust!"

> **vv. 5-6** You will not be afraid of the terror by night, or of the arrow that flies by day; of the pestilence that stalks in darkness, or of the destruction that lays waste at noon.

> **vv. 9-10** For you have made the LORD, my refuge, Even the Most High, your dwelling place. No evil will befall you, nor will any plague come near your tent. For He will give His angels charge concerning you, to guard you in all your ways.

The Continuing *Battle* with Infirmary, Heal Me Lord

As I write this, I feel that the Holy Spirit is speaking to someone who is in the pits of despair. You are not alone. Call upon the name of the Lord! Meditate on Psalm 91. Father, fulfill your Word in Jesus name!

> **Psalm 91:15-16** He will call upon Me, and I will answer him; I will be with him in trouble; I will rescue him and honor him. "With a long life I will satisfy him and let him see My salvation."

My roommate witnessed my nightly episodes and shared his concern for me. I am sure he wondered what kind of roommate he had, especially the first night. He was such an encouragement to me as he was in worse condition than me. He had had a severe stroke four years earlier that resulted in a good portion of his left skull being removed to relieve the pressure on his brain. For some reason he had never had a skull prosthesis placed and had to wear a helmet when out of bed. He just had skin covering his brain on the left side of his head. He was in the hospital having procedures done in preparation to having the skull prosthesis operation and in the rehab center because he was paralyzed on one side of his body.

The first day that I met my roommate, the Holy Spirit spoke and said to be joyful. As my family will tell you, I am a jokester, and he was also. We had a lot of fun together, especially with the nursing and rehab staff. His personality changed when he became irritated, but if I would joke with him, his personality would revert back dramatically. Again, the Holy Spirit brought to mind the power of His Word.

> **1 John 4:18 (KJV)** There is no fear in love; but perfect love casteth out fear: because fear hath torment. He that feareth is not made perfect in love.

FOLLOWING THE *Anointing*: PART II

Proverbs 17:22 (AMP) A happy heart is good medicine *and* a joyful mind causes healing...

Not only did it change my roommate's personality, but it affected me also. The more joyful I was, the better I felt and the better I did physically. The Lord opened doors so that I was able to witness to and pray for him. I am not sure where he is with the Lord and pray that Jesus will continue to reveal Himself to him. I have no doubt that this was a divine appointment, and that this prayer will be fulfilled. **A joyful mind allows healing.**

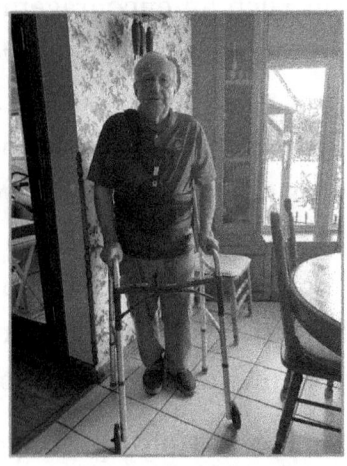

Don in Back Brace after Surgery in Phoenix.

I returned home to Broken Arrow to continue physical therapy after being discharged from the rehab center. I had to wear the back brace while up, was still on pain meds, was quite dependent on others, and had to use a walker, but it was good to be home. I started local outpatient physical therapy three times a week to build up strength in my left leg. It was hard work, but every day I would make slow painful progress. After seeing my neurologist, I was told that my neurological signs were better after surgery with no spasticity, just numbness, weakness, pain, and spasms of the left leg. I felt that that was a confirmation that the Lord was healing my body. It was a daily battle with the enemy who kept telling me I would never get better. Of course, it was hard work, and I had to develop patience knowing that the Lord has more for me to do.

> **Philippians 3:10** that I may know Him and the power of His resurrection and the fellowship of His sufferings, being conformed to His death.

Through sufferings (see appendix on suffering) I have come to know Him and His love in a new and deeper way. I have walked through Psalm 91 and know it is real.

> **Matthew 28:18-20 (AMP)** Jesus came up and said to them, "All authority (all power of absolute rule) in heaven and on earth has been given to Me. Go therefore and make disciples of all the nations [help the people to learn of Me, believe in Me, and obey My words], baptizing them in the name of the Father and of the Son and of the Holy Spirit, teaching them to observe everything that I have commanded you; and lo, I am with you always [remaining with you perpetually—regardless of circumstance, and on every occasion], even to the end of the age."

I have also come to a deeper understanding of the last portion of verse 20: "and lo, I am with you always [remaining with you perpetually—regardless of circumstance, and on every occasion], even to the end of the age." Through difficulties I have come to know that He is **always** with me, no matter what or how I feel. **We are never alone!**

> **PSALM 91** He who dwells in the shelter of the Most High will abide in the shadow of the Almighty. I will say to the Lord, "My refuge and my fortress, My God, in whom I trust!" For it is He who delivers you

FOLLOWING THE *Anointing*: PART II

from the snare of the trapper and from the deadly pestilence. He will cover you with His pinions, and under His wings you may seek refuge; His faithfulness is a shield and bulwark. **You will not be afraid of the terror by night, or of the arrow that flies by day; of the pestilence that stalks in darkness, or of the destruction that lays waste at noon.** A thousand may fall at your side and ten thousand at your right hand, but it shall not approach you. You will only look on with your eyes an see the recompense of the wicked. **For you have made the Lord, my refuge, even the Most High, your dwelling place. No evil will befall you, nor will any plague come near your tent. For He will give His angels charge concerning you, to guard you in all your ways.** They will bear you up in their hands, that you do not strike your foot against a stone. You will tread upon the lion and cobra, the young lion and the serpent you will trample down, **"Because he has loved Me, therefore I will deliver him; I will set him securely on high, because he has known My name. "He will call upon Me, and I will answer him; I will be with him in trouble; I will rescue him and honor him. "With a long life I will satisfy him and let him see My salvation"** (bold emphasis is mine).

The next few weeks after returning home were ones of intensive physical therapy on my left leg as I learned to walk again. I had to use a walker which resulted in pain of the right shoulder that needed to be replaced. Five weeks post-op I developed a lump over the incision site which was an outpouching of the sack covering the spinal cord due to a slow leak of spinal fluid. Since I was not having headaches, the neurosurgeon advised me to leave it alone and it would eventually get smaller, but it could take a while (it disappeared a year and half later). I made good progress in strength until one evening eight weeks after surgery. I was sitting at the kitchen table one evening. Donna was out and I was alone in the house. A large spider was walking across the kitchen floor and without thinking I got up and stomped on it, lost my balance as I was holding onto a chair that

The Continuing *Battle* with Infirmary, Heal Me Lord

tilted over, and I fell to the floor. I had pain in my back and called my son-in-law to come and help me get to bed. Fortunately, I was in my brace, but follow up X-rays showed that I had broken one of the screws holding one of the rods in place. Fortunately, there was still good alignment of the back with the rods still in place. Over the next few weeks, I deteriorated and had to extend the wearing of the brace for a month longer.

In addition, shortly afterward, I was out of the back brace during physical therapy, and while I was laying on a hard therapy table, I lost all sensation to both legs and could not move them. The therapist helped me sit up and some sensation returned, but there was extreme numbness, increased weakness, and difficulty lifting both legs. I deteriorated more and continued wearing the back brace longer. The neurosurgeon advised me to avoid that position as pressure was being exerted on the remaining portion of the spur at T12. I was very discouraged and cried out to God. The pain in my back and shoulders had returned, and it seemed as if I was going backward. Any twisting of my back, especially when getting in and out of a chair or car, resulted in tremendous back and leg pain. I became depressed and had multiple conversations with God. I still had promises of healing, but it did not seem possible. I felt distant from God. I had been used of God in healing, and now I myself again had a tremendous need for healing. (I am sure that one of the major purposes of writing this book was to remind me of what God had done in the past in order to face these current challenges.) All this time my precious wife Donna stood by my side encouraging me, taking me to physical therapy three times a week and all the other medical appointments. Often, I was in pain and not pleasant to be around. At times I was so depressed that I thought it would be better if I was dead. I even thought of committing suicide, but I knew in

FOLLOWING THE *Anointing*: PART II

my heart that was not an option. I quoted scripture to my body and resisted the enemy who was putting these thoughts in my mind.

One day I received an email from YWAM that Joy Dawson had written a book, *My Journey with Jesus*,[18] and felt the Holy Spirit nudge me to read it. I obtained the book and was blessed. Joy was an international speaker and very influential leader of YWAM. I had heard her speak multiple times and was impressed by her walk with God and hearing His voice. She was probably one of the most intense people I have ever met. I knew that she had not been traveling or teaching for several years. As I read her book, I discovered that she had spinal surgery that had not gone well, and she essentially had been an invalid for approximately twenty-seven years because of pain. During that difficult time, she received words of healing from the Lord and believed for it, even at the time of writing her book at the age of ninety-six. This really spoke to me. Here I was six months after surgery and discouraged because I had not fully recovered. Forgive me, Lord, for my unbelief. I wrote her a note thanking her for how much I was encouraged by her book. She sent me a nice card back thanking me and claiming the following scripture for me. The next year she went home to the Lord where she received her healing.

1 Timothy 4:17 But the Lord stood by me and gave me strength.

Thank you, Lord, for the fulfillment of your promises in my life and forgive me of my unbelief. I now wait for the fulfillment of Your Word to me, that I have more to do for you. **Is that where you are also at in your life? Where are you on the road to Emmaus? Let Jesus walk beside you.**

The X-rays and CT scan at six months post-op showed good alignment, and I eventually was able to come out of my brace.

The Continuing *Battle* with Infirmary, Heal Me Lord

Every day I became stronger, but it was a long, slow process, and at times my left leg felt numb and dead (still does). I progressed from walking with a walker to a cane several months later when I was more stable. I now walk independently in our home but continue to use the cane when out of the house. I am still believing God for the fulfillment of Hebrews 12:12-13. The physical problems continue to be one of the greatest struggles of my life as well as not being able to be independent and needing the help of others.

Two years after the back surgery I had a frozen shoulder replaced. I finally was able to walk with a cane without shoulder pain and progressed in my physical therapy. Just when I thought the rehab was over, my right hip (the side which had sustained the left weak leg) gave out. I had severe arthritic changes in the joint and was walking bone on bone. I had to have a total hip replacement. One and a half years after the shoulder replacement, an abscess developed in it. I had to go through surgery again with debridement, removal of the apparatus, and replacement. As I write today, I am on long-term antibiotic therapy suffering the side effect from the drugs.

So discouraging – will it ever end? Lord, why won't you heal me supernaturally? Do I lack faith? I have seen your power, and I have felt it. I had even taught about the supernatural healing power of God and also about the combination of prayer and medicine. After the hip replacement and shoulder redo, it was like I was starting all over again having more physical therapy. I kept asking the Lord if the pain would ever stop. I prayed and prayed confessing the words he had given me in the past. Then one day as I was alone in the house, spontaneously I spoke out loud in tongues for a few minutes. I had no control over what I was speaking, and it was the same as when I gave the message in tongues in Malaysia. When finished speaking in tongues, in English the Lord spoke to me in my mind and again said that He was not through with me, that I had more to do for Him. He also said that I would see and be involved in the next release of His Spirit. Thank you, Lord, while struggling and in pain, you confirm you have a purpose for my life. I will fight through for I know that you are still with me. Yes and Amen, Lord, I will be able walk again and to minister in your name. "Bring it to pass in Jesus's name!"

CHAPTER 21

Suffering

As I was struggling through the above situation, I came across a description of a book in *Christianity Today* by Russ Ramsey entitled *Stuck*.[19] It is the story of a pastor who was struck by a bacterial infection that destroyed his mitral valve, sending him into heart failure requiring open heart surgery. He describes the same emotions that I am going through as he faced the possibilities of death and came to look at the world through the eyes of the afflicted, just as I have. He fought fear, anger, depression, and loss yet experienced grace through suffering that filled him with a hope and hunger for the life to come. I cried through the book and how it ministered to me that I am not alone in my walk. He made a profound statement that "historically, God deals with those He loves by breaking them. It is because of His lovingkindness that He moves me always deeper into a posture of dependence."[20] How I understand this scripture!

> **Psalm 23:4** Even though I walk through the valley of the shadow of death, I fear no evil, for You are with me; Your rod and Your staff, they comfort me.

FOLLOWING THE *Anointing*: PART II

Isn't interesting how God brought Joy Dawson's[18] and Russ Ransey's[19] books across my paths at just the right time that I needed to be encouraged? Yes, I don't know how (perhaps it is this book), but I will fulfill what God has left for me to do here on earth. I know Him each day at a deeper level than the day before. Lord, show me how to be more dependent upon You and to hear your voice clearly. **Are you also struggling today? If so, then walk with me and the Lord through these next few pages and the appendix.** Before and during my current struggles, the Holy Spirit spoke to me via different means:

1. A word: **Hebrews 12:12-13** Therefore, strengthen the hands that are weak and the knees that are feeble, and make straight paths for your feet, so that the limb which is lame may not be put out of joint, but rather be healed.

2. Prophetic word from three different men of God that I had more to do for Him.

3. A vision of the Lord Jesus Christ in which He said that I had not completed my assigned tasks for Him.

4. A spontaneous message in tongues after shoulder and hip surgery as I was praying where the Lord spoke to me and again said again that He was not through with me and I had more to do for Him. I would see and be involved the next release of His Spirit.

I know His power through ministry and have insight into the power of His resurrection after seeing someone clinically dead raised up, yet I needed to know Him in a deeper way through the **"fellowship of His suffering."** In my continuing battles with infirmary, I have come to an understanding of "His suffering." Through suffering I have felt despair and loneliness. At my lowest point He appeared to me and gave me hope. I have felt His healing touch through medical science and through His supernatural power. **Are you walking through the fellowship of suffering?** If that is you, praise Him for He wants to give you a revelation of His love and His purpose for your life. What the enemy meant for evil God will turn around to His glory. **You will know God in a new way so that through His love you can take others into His presence** (see appendix on Suffering). Even when you are weak, through His love, acceptance, and anointing, as you share the truths of His Word, you take people into His presence. **This is your purpose in life – to take others into His presence** (see Chapter 22 on Purpose of Your Anointing from God), which heals not only those with whom you share but also yourself.

> **1 Thessalonians 5:23** Now may the God of peace Himself sanctify you entirely; and may your spirit and soul and body be kept complete, without blame at the coming of our Lord Jesus Christ.

God will sustain you through your struggles as you complete His tasks for you. These are His promises for you:

> **James 1:2-4** Consider it all joy, my brethren, when you encounter various trials, knowing that the testing of your faith produces endurance. And let endurance have its perfect result, so that you may be perfect and complete, lacking in nothing.

> **1 Peter 1:6-8** In this you greatly rejoice, even though now for a little while, if necessary, you have been distressed by various trials, so that the proof of your faith, being more precious than gold which is perishable, even though tested by fire, may be found to result in praise and glory and honor at the revelation of Jesus Christ; and though you have not seen Him, you love Him, and though you do not see Him now,

but believe in Him, you greatly rejoice with joy inexpressible and full of glory, obtaining as the outcome of your faith the salvation of your souls.

1 Peter 5:10 After you have suffered for a little while, the God of all grace, who called you to His eternal glory in Christ, will Himself perfect, confirm, strengthen, and establish you.

CHAPTER 22

Purpose of Your *Anointing* from God

    I thought I was finished, but I believe the Holy Spirit would have me add these few paragraphs about the purpose of the anointing of God in your life even with struggles and suffering. **Whatever your situation is in life, you are to lead others into His presence.** When the Lord uses you in healing by the laying on of hands for physical healing, speaking a word of knowledge that results in inner healing, moving in His authority to give deliverance from demonic forces, or proclaiming the public word that He has given you, **the purpose of His anointing is to take the individual(s) into the presence of God.** It is His presence (glory) that changes lives and brings healing. **Through following His anointing, we learn how to be a vessel of His glory.** It is no different than when Solomon dedicated the temple.

    2 Chronicles 5:11-14 When the priests came out from the holy place (for all the priests who were present had sanctified themselves,

FOLLOWING THE *Anointing*: PART II

without regard to divisions), and all the Levitical singers, Asaph, Heman, Jeduthun, and their sons and kinsmen, clothed in fine linen, with cymbals, harps, and lyres, standing east of the altar, and with them 120 priests blowing trumpets in unison when the trumpeters and the singers were to make themselves heard with one voice to praise and to glorify the LORD, and when they raised their voices accompanied by trumpets, cymbals, and other musical instruments, and when they praised the LORD saying, "He indeed is good for His kindness is everlasting," then the house, the house of the LORD, was filled with a cloud, so that the priests could not rise to minister because of the cloud, for the glory of the LORD filled the house of God.

2 Chronicles 7:1 Now when Solomon had finished praying, fire came down from heaven and consumed the burnt offering and the sacrifices, and the glory of the LORD filled the house.

1 Corinthians 6:19 Or do you not know that your body is a temple of the Holy Spirit who is in you, whom you have from God, and that you are not your own?

God's glory, His presence, is filling His temple, our bodies! This is what heals and changes lives. That is why His charge to the disciples and to you is:

Mark 16:15-20 And He said to them, "Go into all the world and preach the gospel to all creation. The one who has believed and has been baptized will be saved; but the one who has not believed will be condemned. These signs will accompany those who have believed: in My name they will cast out demons, they will speak with new tongues; they will pick up serpents, and if they drink any deadly poison, it will not harm them; they will lay hands on the sick, and they will recover." So then, when the Lord Jesus had spoken to them, He was received up into heaven and sat down at the right hand of God. And they went out and preached everywhere, **while the Lord worked with them,**

Purpose of Your *Anointing* from God

and confirmed the word by the signs that followed (bold emphasis is mine).

God promise to you and me is the same today. As we followed the voice of the Holy Spirit, His anointing, He will confirm His Word with signs as His glory is manifested to whom we minister. It may even be during times of weakness, suffering, or struggles in our life as we acknowledge and praise Him.

> **1 Timothy 1:15-17** It is a trustworthy statement, deserving full acceptance, that Christ Jesus came into the world to save sinners, among whom I am foremost. Yet for this reason I found mercy, so that in me as the foremost sinner Jesus Christ might demonstrate His perfect patience as an example for those who would believe in Him for eternal life. Now to the King eternal, immortal, invisible, **the only God, be honor and glory forever and ever.** Amen (bold emphasis is mine).

Part I[1] and this Part II of our story may well be the fulfillment of the prophetic words given above that I had more to do for Him. As we conclude our story, Donna and I want to thank you for walking with us in our journey with God that is not finished. We pray that this part of our journey dealing with a marketplace ministry gives Him glory as will your journey with Him. We invite you to come to know Him in a new way as we have. We pray that you will be obedient to follow His anointing for your life's Journey.

> **1 John 2:27** And as for you, the anointing which you received from Him remains in you, and you have no need for anyone to teach you; but as **His anointing teaches you about all things**, and is true and is not a lie, and just as it has taught you, you remain in Him (bold emphasis is mine).

Appendix

Often during devotion time or as I was praying about a service, the Lord would bring various scriptures to mind. Then as I would medicate on them, a teaching or message would come often combined with a personal testimony. Other times, the Lord would only give me a scripture with which to start, and then as I spoke, He would bring various incidents in my life to mind along with other scriptures. The appendix of part one of our story[1] lists some of these teachings and messages. Part two of our story deals with ministry opportunities while working in the marketplace as a Christian physician. With the ministry also came challenging struggles and suffering. The following appendix is the one I am walking through now, growing in the Lord through suffering and struggles.

STRUGGLING, SUFFERING, AND GROWING IN THE LORD[21,22]

As we approach the end of our story of following God's anointing part two, I feel compelled to discuss suffering and its effect upon my life. If you are reading this, then you may be in a similar situation.

FOLLOWING THE *Anointing*: PART II

While it is so easy to rejoice about the power and the anointing of God plus the walk of faith, **I submit to you that you cannot fully appreciate Him in His fullness without understanding the fellowship of suffering.** While I quoted Philippians 3:14-15 earlier, look at previous verses in this chapter.

> **Philippians 3:8-11 (MSG)** Yes, all the things I once thought were so important are gone from my life. Compared to the high privilege of knowing Christ Jesus as my Master, firsthand, everything I once thought I had going for me is insignificant – dog dung. I've dumped it all in the trash so that I could embrace Christ and be embraced by him. I didn't want some petty, inferior brand of righteousness that comes from keeping a list of rules when I could get the robust kind that comes from trusting Christ – God's righteousness.
>
> **I gave up all that inferior stuff so I could know Christ personally, experience his resurrection power, be a partner in his suffering, and go all the way with him to death itself. If there was any way to get in on the resurrection from the dead, I wanted to do it** (bold emphasis is mine).

To be a partner in His suffering, even death, is to identify with Him more fully. As I reflect on my life, I came to know Him intimately as my Lord after He healed my lower back. He healed me and filled me with the Holy Spirit even when I did not believe in it because I had never been taught that it existed today. As I flowed in His anointing, I witnessed Him touch others. **Once you experience the power of God working through you, you are never the same.** Earlier in my walk my hands would shake under the anointing so I would know that He was with me, but now I have the confidence that He is with me at all times. All I have to do is to be sensitive to His Holy Spirit.

Appendix

I was challenged late in life with so much back and neurological pain that I wanted to die. Yet, I saw Jesus in my hospital room. I looked into His eyes and felt peace go through my body. In retrospect, I would like to have not had the suffering. I have to be honest and say that I have come to know Him more through suffering to a greater depth than during the glorious times of ministry. Are we fulfilling "Job type experiences" in our lives through suffering? With this thought in mind, let's look at some additional biblical statements about suffering.

> **Matthew 10:38 (AMP)** "And he who does not take up his cross and follow Me [cleave steadfastly to Me, conforming wholly to My example in living and, if need be, in dying also] is not worthy of Me."

> **Philippians 3:10** that I may know Him and the power of His resurrection and the fellowship of His sufferings, being conformed to His death.

> **Acts 20:24** I consider my life worth nothing to me, if only I may finish the race and complete the task the Lord Jesus has given to me — the task of testifying to the gospel of God's grace.

> **Hebrews 12:1-3** Therefore, since we have so great a cloud of witnesses surrounding us, let us also lay aside every encumbrance and the sin which so easily entangles us, and let us run with endurance the race that is set before us, fixing our eyes on Jesus, the author and perfecter of faith, who for the joy set before Him endured the cross, despising the shame, and has sat down at the right hand of the throne of God. For consider Him who has endured such hostility by sinners against Himself, so that you will not grow weary and lose heart.

In my walk of following His anointing, suffering seems to be a major factor. Still, I preach and share about a good God that does good things for His people. How can I believe that He has me suffer in order to know Him? My rationale mind then would conclude that God may be the source of my suffering, but scripture says that He is not the source. He does allow them to come, however.

> **James 1:2-4 (MSG)** Consider it a sheer gift, friends, when tests and challenges come at you from all sides. You know that under pressure, your faith-life is forced into the open and shows its true colors. So, don't try to get out of anything prematurely. Let it do its work, so you become mature and well-developed, not deficient in any way.

Through trials and suffering you can mature spiritually. At this point, I remember preaching about Job in Malaysia where God's supernatural power was so evident. I remember reading the following verse in Job.

> **Job 1:8** The LORD said to Satan, "Have you considered My servant Job? For there is no one like him on the earth, a blameless and upright man, fearing God and turning away from evil."

I remember making the statement, "I wonder would God have enough confidence in Don Tredway to say to the enemy, 'Have you considered my servant Don Tredway?', just as He did Job?" Am I walking out those words today? I should be paralyzed from the waist down, but I am a walking miracle because scripture also says

> **2 Peter 2:9** then the Lord knows how to rescue the godly from temptation, and to keep the unrighteous under punishment for the day of judgment.

In a book we used in the Medical DTS (MEDTS) written by a long-term medical missionary, Dr. Fountain, is a chapter addressing the subject of "Illness: Tragedy or Challenge?"[21] Could illness also

Appendix

be a challenge to grow in Him? In addition, a former professor at Oral Roberts University, Dr. Matthew, has an interesting chapter, "A Pastoral View of Pain and Suffering," where he summarizes various views of suffering.[22] I remember my Pastor Bob Yandian[2] saying that **"God's power to rebuild is always greater than the power of destruction."** What a profound statement.

I also remember the relationship that David had with God. David is often quoted as being the man after God's heart. When things went wrong in his life, he would go to his knees and pray, "Oh God where have I failed you, where have I sinned?" If God revealed anything he would confess and get his life right with God and go on. If God did not reveal anything, then he would go on in the strength of who he was in God. Look how much he suffered, some from his own making and sin but other times from the attacks of the enemy, friends, and family. As you read the Psalms, you get an understanding of David's unique relationship with God.

> **1 Peter 2:20** For what credit is there if, when you sin and are harshly treated, you endure it with patience? But if when you do what is right and suffer for it you patiently endure it, this finds favor with God.

Suffering can come to us when we are either in or out of the will of God. Unfortunately, we are never exempt from suffering because of the broken world in which we live in due to Adam's original sin. But God is always with His children during difficult times just as He was with Jesus in Gethsemane. God will never desert you nor forsake you.

> **Hebrews 13:5 (AMP)** ...for He has said, "I WILL NEVER [under any circumstances] DESERT YOU [nor give you up nor leave you without support, nor will I in any degree leave you helpless], NOR WILL I

FOLLOWING THE *Anointing*: PART II

FORSAKE or LET YOU DOWN or RELAX MY HOLD ON YOU [assuredly not]!"

1 Corinthians 10:13 (MSG) No test or temptation that comes your way is beyond the course of what others have had to face. All you need to remember is that God will never let you down; he'll never let you be pushed past your limit; he'll always be there to help you come through it.

I also know that some of my suffering has come from ignorance because I did not understand His Word or follow His commands. But I know that I am loved of God and can identify with this Psalm.

Psalm 34:19 Many are the afflictions of the righteous, But the LORD delivers him out of them all.

Matthew 5:11-12 "Blessed are you when people insult you and persecute you and falsely say all kinds of evil against you because of Me. Rejoice and be glad, for your reward in heaven is great; for in the same way, they persecuted the prophets who were before you."

Jesus certainly suffered while in the will of God, and that is an important part of our identity in Him. Jesus is our example in suffering how to handle it.

1 Peter 2:21-25 For you have been called for this purpose, since Christ also suffered for you, leaving you an example for you to follow in His steps, **who committed no sin, nor was any deceit in His mouth**; and while being reviled, He did not revile in return; while suffering, He uttered no threats, but kept entrusting Himself to Him who judges righteously; and He Himself bore our sins in His body on the cross, so that we might die to sin and live to righteousness; for by His wounds you were healed. For you were continually straying like sheep, but

Appendix

now you have returned to the Shepherd and Guardian of your souls (bold emphasis is mine).

As difficult as it is for me to accept, suffering has been and is an important part of my walk with God. Often, we want the anointing, the excitement, fulfillment, and sometimes even the acclaim. The fellowship of suffering has taught me the extent and breath of His love. I probably could not have accepted that statement a few years ago, but now I know that I know.

Romans 4:20 yet, with respect to the promise of God, he did not waver in unbelief but grew strong in faith, giving glory to God…

James 1:2-3 Consider it all joy, my brethren, when you encounter various trials, knowing that the testing of your faith produces endurance.

Philippians 1:29 For to you it has been granted for Christ's sake, not only to believe in Him, but also to suffer for His sake, experiencing the same conflict which you saw in me, and now hear to be in me.

Look at all that Paul accomplished through suffering and what he wrote in Philippians.

Philippines 1:12-14 Now I want you to know, brethren, that my circumstances have turned out for the greater progress of the gospel, so that my imprisonment in the cause of Christ has become well known throughout the whole praetorian guard and to everyone else, and that most of the brethren, trusting in the Lord because of my imprisonment, have far more courage to speak the word of God without fear.

I also cannot but wonder if my thorn in the flesh is my back problems.

FOLLOWING THE *Anointing*: PART II

> **2 Corinthians 12:7-10** Because of the surpassing greatness of the revelations, for this reason, to keep me from exalting myself, there was given me a thorn in the flesh, a messenger of Satan to torment me—to keep me from exalting myself! Concerning this I implored the Lord three times that it might leave me. And He has said to me, "My grace is sufficient for you, for power is perfected in weakness." Most gladly, therefore, I will rather boast about my weaknesses, so that the power of Christ may dwell in me. Therefore, I am well content with weaknesses, with insults, with distresses, with persecutions, with difficulties, for Christ's sake; for when I am weak, then I am strong.

Even though my back conditions may well be a thorn in the flesh, through it I have come to know the Lord Jesus Christ in an intimate way. This relationship started with my first healing[1] and continues as I walk through my current challenges. I have no doubt of His healing nature.

God will sustain you also through your struggles as you complete His tasks for you. These are His promises for you:

> **James 1:2-4** Consider it all joy, my brethren, when you encounter various trials, knowing that the testing of your faith produces endurance. And let endurance have its perfect result, so that you may be perfect and complete, lacking in nothing.

> **1 Peter 1:6-8** In this you greatly rejoice, even though now for a little while, if necessary, you have been distressed by various trials, so that the proof of your faith, being more precious than gold which is perishable, even though tested by fire, may be found to result in praise and glory and honor at the revelation of Jesus Christ; and though you have not seen Him, you love Him, and though you do not see Him now, but believe in Him, you greatly rejoice with joy inexpressible and full of glory, obtaining as the outcome of your faith the salvation of your souls.

Appendix

1 Peter 5:10 After you have suffered for a little while, the God of all grace, who called you to His eternal glory in Christ, will Himself perfect, confirm, strengthen, and establish you.

Psalm 103:5 Who satisfies your years with good things, So that your youth is renewed like the eagle.

1 John 2:27 And as for you, the anointing which you received from Him remains in you, and you have no need for anyone to teach you; but as **His anointing teaches you about all things**, and is true and is not a lie, and just as it has taught you, you remain in Him (bold emphasis is mine).

Is this you today? Rejoice in the Lord Jesus Christ and praise Him at all times. As you praise Him, through your weakness, He will use you to take others into His presence. May you grow in Him as you follow His anointing in all its manifestations in your life.

Bibliography

1. Tredway, Donald and Donna. *Following the Anointing, Part I.* Tulsa, OK: Insight International, 2024.

2. "Bob Yandian Ministries." https://www.bobyandian.com/.

3. Nouwen, Henri JM. *The Return of the Prodigal Son.* New York, NY: Doubleday, 1992.

4. Frost, Jack. *Experiencing Father's Embrace.* Lake Mary, FL: Charisma House, 2002.

5. Frost, Jack. *Experiencing Father's Embrace Workbook.* Conway, SC: Father's House Productions, Inc., 2002.

6. McClung Jr., Floyd. *The Father Heart of God.* Harvest House Publishers. Eugene, Oregon, 1985.

7. Wayne, Jacobsen. *He Loves Me.* Newbury Park, CA: Windblown Media, 2007.

8. Tredway DR, Kirsch WM, Zhu YH, Weber K, Norburg M, Saukel GW, and Seraj I. A new concept for reanastomoses of the fallopian tube. Fertil and Steril 62:624-9, 1994.

9. Peretti, Frank. *This Present Darkness.* New York, NY: Howard Books, 2003.

10. L.B.E. Cowman and Jim Reimann. *Streams in the Desert.* Zondervan, Grand Rapids, MI, 1997

11. Thompson, Dr. Bruce and Barbara. *Walls of My Heart.* Crown Ministries International, Euclid, MN, 1989.

12. "Starseite." Stiftung Schleife. https://www.schleife.ch/.

13. Payne, Leanne. *The Broken Image: Restoring Personal Wholeness through Healing Prayer*. Grand Rapids, MI: Baker Books, 1981,1996.

14. Payne, Leanne. *Restoring the Christian Soul: Overcoming Barriers to Completion in Christ through Healing Prayer*. Grand Rapids, MI: Baker Books, 1991.

15. Lanier, Sarah A. *Foreign to Familiar*. Hagerstown, MD: McDougal Publishing, 2010.

16. Stone, Perry. *Exposing Satan's Playbook: The secrets and strategies Satan hopes you never discover*. Charisma House, 2012.

17. Eckhardt, John. *Deliverance and Spiritual Warfare Manual*. Lake Mary FL: Charisma House, 2014

18. Dawson, Joy. *My Journey with Jesus*. Lake View Terrace, CA: Self-published, 2021.

19. Ramsey, Russ. *Struck*. Downers Grove, Il: InterVarsity Press, 2017.

20. Ramsey, Russ. *Struck*, 105-106. Downers Grove, Il: InterVarsity Press, 2017.

21. Fountain, Daniel E. "Illness: Tragedy or Challenge?" Chapter. In *God, Medicine & Miracles*, 191. Colorado Springs, CO: Waterbrook Press, 1999.

22. Matthew, Thomson K. "A Pastoral View of Pain and Suffering" Chapter. In *Ministry Between Miracles*, 113. Kottayam, Kerala, India: GoodNews Books, 2020.

Author Contact

Resurrection Ministries, Inc.

Donald Tredway: drtreds@aol.com

Donna Tredway: ddtreds@aol.com

Notes

Notes

Notes

Notes

www.ingramcontent.com/pod-product-compliance
Lightning Source LLC
Chambersburg PA
CBHW062154080426
42734CB00010B/1690